A. (Antoine) Touron,
Pierre-Franc

ois-Xavier de Charlevoix

Opening chapter of American missionary history

Life of Bartholomew de Las Casas

A. (Antoine) Touron,
Pierre-Franc

ois-Xavier de Charlevoix

Opening chapter of American missionary history
Life of Bartholomew de Las Casas

ISBN/EAN: 9783741178627

Manufactured in Europe, USA, Canada, Australia, Japa

Cover: Foto ©Andreas Hilbeck / pixelio.de

Manufactured and distributed by brebook publishing software (www.brebook.com)

A. (Antoine) Touron,
Pierre-Franc

ois-Xavier de Charlevoix

Opening chapter of American missionary history

Opening Chapter of American Missionary History.

LIFE

OF

Bartholomew de Las Casas,

OF THE ORDER OF ST. DOMINIC, PROTECTOR-GENERAL OF THE
INDIANS AND FIRST BISHOP OF CHIAPA IN MEXICO.

Compiled from the French of Touron and Charlevoix.

WITH AN APPENDIX FROM THE WRITINGS OF
WASHINGTON IRVING, ETC.

BY ONE OF THE DOMINICAN FATHERS OF NEW YORK.

NEW YORK:
P. O'SHEA, 27 BARCLAY STREET.
1871.

Translator's Preface.

On the 12th of October, 1492, Columbus first set foot upon the shores of the New World. He was received by its inhabitants with friendship and confidence. The great discoverer always treated them with justice and respect; but it was his misfortune to be followed by men who ignored in their regard every principle of justice, and looked upon them as a totally inferior race, hardly capable of any degree of civilization. Provocation to deeds of violence furnished occasions in abundance for their destruction or enslavement; and the records of human cruelty scarcely furnish details more revolting than the general conduct of the first Spanish settlers towards the natives of the West India Islands. It is true that the English settlers of North America cannot show a clear record on the same subject—on the contrary, the policy of extermination has been acted upon by them with the most relentless cruelty and consistent pertinacity; but the sins of one nation can form no excuse for those of another.

What we wish to prove by the publication of this translation is, that whilst in the one case hardly a name remarkable in history stands upon the side of justice and humanity, in the other a phalanx of courageous men, distinguished both for learning and for virtue, cease not for a whole century to preach and write and labor for the conversion and preservation of this unhappy race; and, failing sometimes in their noble efforts, they give to the world, with the boldest freedom, the fullest details respecting the injustice and inhumanity of their own countrymen.

All the Dominican Fathers who accompanied or followed the first colonists to the Indies stand prominently forward in this noble conflict. Not one of them failed to cover with the mantle of his protection the poor natives of this land; not one discordant note is heard in the grand anthem of pity that never ceased to be sung in favor of the Indian race by the sons of St. Dominic.

But among them all we hear one voice above the rest. We hear it for seventy years. We hear it in St. Domingo, in Cuba, on the whole north coast of South America; we hear it in

Mexico, in Guatemala, in Peru; we hear it in the wildest forests, in the rudest mountain fastnesses, in the most unhealthy swamps, along the most remote rivers, in the wildest valleys; we hear it not only among the savage tribes of America but also at the court of King Ferdinand in Spain; it is listened to with respect by the renowned Ximenes who was regent of Spain after the death of Ferdinand; it is a voice of thunder in the councils of Charles V., and it is not hushed in death till long in the reign of Philip II. The one unceasing strain of that heavenly voice is justice and mercy to the Indians—the curse of God in this life and eternal torments in the future to those Spaniards who would violate in their regard the rights of men. That voice of Christian mercy, that indomitable energy in doing good, is the subject of this little volume.

[The sketch of the life of Las Casas here presented to American readers is intended only to give the general outlines of his character.] But it is thoroughly reliable in an historical point of view, and will supply a much-needed chapter in the missionary history of America. In years to come some one competent to the task, and having sufficient time for the work, will give to the world, it is hoped, a full life of Las Casas. Till then we recommend to Christian readers in general the following brief notice of a Christian hero principally taken from the writings of the great historian Charlevoix and from those of Touron, the biographer of "Illustrious Dominicans."

Special attention is also called to the appendix in which our own historian Irving, himself so much indebted to Las Casas for the matter out of which to form one of his most valuable works, triumphantly defends that venerable man from a charge that is too commonly made against him.

CONTENTS.

CHAPTER I.

Family of Las Casas.—His Birth.—His knowledge of the Indian Tongue.—His Voyage to America.—His career in the Island of Cuba...... 9

CHAPTER II.

His Friendship for the Dominican Friars.—The Repartimientos, or Governmental System of the Colonies.—Fathers Montesino and Cordova.—Their Disputes with the Spanish Colonists respecting their injustice to the Natives.—The affair brought before King Ferdinand in Spain.—Decrees in favor of the Indians....................... 13

CHAPTER III.

Joy of Las Casas over the success of Montesino.—Bad faith of the Authorities in St. Domingo and coldness of King Ferdinand.—Las Casas publishes the decrees himself.—Two of the Dominican Fathers depart for the Coast of Cumana where they are successful in converting the Natives.—The perfidy of a Spanish Captain exasperates the Indians and causes the death of the two Fathers.—Las Casas labors successfully among the Natives of Cuba.—Continued cruelties of the Colonists and departure of Las Casas to Spain.—He is promised an Audience.—Death of the King................................. 27

CHAPTER IV.

Las Casas pleads for the Indians before Cardinal Ximenes.—Enforcement of the old regulations and enactment of new ones.—Commissioners appointed to go to the West Indies in order to protect the native population.—Las Casas is appointed Protector-General of the Indians.—Means are still contrived to counteract his designs and he returns to Spain,... 41

CONTENTS.

CHAPTER V.

Las Casas at the Court of Charles V.—His triumphant appeal before the Emperor and the Royal Audience in favor of the Indians.—He is seconded by a Franciscan Friar and by Diego Columbus, Admiral of the Indies.—The former decrees in favor of the Indians confirmed.—Other abuses corrected.—Las Casas obtains a charter for a certain territory where he is to establish an Indian settlement according to his own plan. 46

CHAPTER VI.

Further troubles on the Coast of Cumana.—Las Casas establishes a Colony there which is ruined by the imprudence of his Lieutenant in his absence. 57

CHAPTER VII.

Las Casas becomes a Dominican.—Lives eight years in retirement.—Becomes Prior of the Convent of St. Domingo.—Goes to Spain to obtain from Charles V. regulations favorable to the Indians of Mexico and Peru recently conquered by Cortez and Pizarro.—History of the Cacique Henry. 68

CHAPTER VIII.

Las Casas visits Mexico, Peru and other provinces to publish in them the decrees of the Emperor in favor of the Indians.—With some of his brother Dominicans he conquers to the faith the "Land of War."—He goes to Spain again.—Is appointed first Bishop of Chiapa.—His difficulties as Bishop.—Resigns his See.—Returns to Spain for the last time.—His controversy with Sepulveda.—His Death. 86

APPENDIX.

I. Containing an extract from Irving's Life of Columbus, and showing the views of Las Casas on negro slavery. 105

II. Is the Apostolic of Pope Paul III. declaring the Indians to be capable of Christian instruction and forbidding them to be deprived of their liberty. 119

LIFE OF BARTHOLOMEW DE LAS CASAS.

CHAPTER I.

HIS FAMILY.—HIS BIRTH.—HIS KNOWLEDGE OF THE INDIAN TONGUE.—HIS VOYAGE TO AMERICA.—HIS CAREER IN THE ISLAND OF CUBA.

ALL the historians who have given us any account of the conquests of the Spaniards in the West Indies, or of their cruelties towards the native inhabitants, have also made honorable mention of the noble charity and ardent zeal of Bartholomew de Las Casas. He is held up to our admiration as a holy personage; zealous, intrepid and indefatigable; equally celebrated in the Old World and in the New.

The family of Las Casas, (originally Caseus) was of French origin. His ancestors passed into Spain in the days of Ferdinand, surnamed the *Saint;* they distinguished themselves in the wars against the Moors, particularly at the siege of Seville, which city Ferdinand rescued from these infidels in 1247. They obtained lordly possessions in the conquered territory, and ever sustained with credit the dignity of their well-merited position. Bartholomew was born at Seville in the beginning of the remarkable reign of Ferdinand and Isabella in 1474. Some writers assert that, at the age of nineteen years, he accompanied his father, Don Antonio Las Casas, on his voyage to America with Columbus in 1493. On his return to Spain he resumed his studies in the university of Salamanca, where he made honorable progress not only in theology, but also in canon and civil law. His writings certainly bear unquestionable evidence of his erudition.

When the generous Queen Isabella, with feelings of virtuous indignation, published a decree setting free those Indians who had been brought as slaves into Spain, Las Casas, joyfully availing himself of the law, immediately liberated an Indian that had been given him by his father; and sent him back to his native land loaded with presents. He had taken special care to have him instructed in the Christian religion, and conceived from that time for the Indians those tender sentiments of compassion which distinguished him in later years. It is not certain whether it was during his visit to America, as some supposed, or from this captive Indian that he obtained a thorough knowledge of the Indian language. The certain fact of this acquirement gave him a decided superiority over his countrymen in treating with the natives of America.

Probably it was this special qualification that recommended him to the notice of Don Nicholas D'Ovando, knight of Alcantara, who, having been appointed by the court of Castile viceroy of Hispaniola or St. Domingo, was accompanied by Las Casas on his voyage thither in 1502. Las Casas may even then have been in *sacred* orders, but he was not ordained priest till his arrival in America.*

The year after his arrival he received letters of invitation from Diego Velasquez, governor of the island of Cuba, to make that island the theatre of his usefulness and zeal. Las Casas having consented to this request obtained a place in the governor's council and an appointment as pastor of Zaguarama. Authors generally agree that these dignities were conferred upon him only in order that, through his knowl-

---

* It is very generally supposed that he was the first priest ordained on the American Continent.

edge of the Indian dialect, he might gain the confidence of the natives, and, under pretence of defending them, deprive them of their liberty. It seems also that, not perceiving at first the baseness of the plot, or perhaps reluctant to give offence to a benefactor, he became, for a time, the tool of his cupidity. He soon discovered his error, and, always faithful to the promptings of justice, regarded with horror the cruelties inflicted with impunity upon a people who had fallen into the most wretched slavery solely because they had been the rightful owners of the very soil they were now forced to cultivate for the benefit of others. He openly condemned the injustice of his countrymen; he condemned himself for having appeared, even unconsciously, to sanction it; he resigned his dignities; and resolved, from that moment, to suffer all hardships and brave all dangers in order to insure the freedom of the natives and free them from ruthless tyranny.

CHAPTER II.

HIS FRIENDSHIP FOR THE DOMINICAN FRIARS—THE REPARTIMIENTOS OR GOVERNMENTAL SYSTEM OF THE COLONIES.—FATHERS MONTESINO AND CORDOVA.—THEIR DISPUTES WITH THE SPANISH COLONISTS RESPECTING THEIR INJUSTICE TO THE NATIVES.—THE AFFAIR BROUGHT BEFORE KING FERDINAND IN SPAIN.—DECREES IN FAVOR OF THE INDIANS.

HE soon formed a very close friendship with certain Dominican Fathers lately established in the island of Hispaniola, who used every exertion to confirm him in his good resolution and induce him to use all his influence to remove what they regarded as the greatest obstacle to the conversion of the natives. Nothing contributed so much to render the preaching of the Gospel contemptible and its ministers odious in their eyes as the injuries they received at the hands of the Spaniards. The ministers of religion, it is true, resisted these proceedings with great zeal; but the preachers were of the same nation as the conquerers, and the simple natives writhing under oppression made little distinction between them. To put an end to this scandal and render honorable the ministry of those who exposed themselves to all dangers to gain souls to Christ, it was necessary in the first place to put a restraint upon cupidity and to abolish a number of abuses introduced and almost consecrated by avarice.

One of the principal of these and the most difficult to correct was the system of repartimientos, which we shall here explain.

Under the terms *repartimiento, distribution, command* or *concession* were comprehended certain districts of country which the Castilian noblemen appropriated to themselves, each according to his own discretion or the will of the governor. To each repartimiento was also assigned a certain number of Indians who were to cultivate the lands and labor in the mines for the benefit of their new masters. The islanders, who from masters had become slaves, were so oppressed by the labor and fatigue to which they were totally unaccustomed that many sunk in death under the weight of their afflictions. Having lost their property and then their liberty, they now lost life itself. No distinction was made as to age, sex or condition; young children, tender maidens, women of quality as well as men were obliged to cultivate the soil, dig in the mines, and remain several hours together in the rivers to pick up precious stones. The Caciques, or native chieftains, received no better treatment. The oppression increased daily either on account of the smallness of the number that mortality had spared or on account of the great multiplication of Spanish adventurers. At first only the chief officers who had borne arms on American soil could expect the government of repartimientos; afterwards it was only necessary to cross the seas to become possessed of the riches of a country which belonged, it was said, by right of conquest to Spain. Most of the nobles and ministers of the Castilian court thought fit to solicit repartimientos from the king, and their request was seldom refused. Thus it often happened that a Castilian nobleman, without leaving home, without any trouble or expense on his part, found himself suddenly possessed of several leagues of territory in the New World to which were attached several thousand Indian slaves who were to enrich these lands by the sweat of their brow. Many of these nobles never being able to visit their possessions were obliged to appoint agents who were called sometimes *procurators* and sometimes *intendants*. These were often persons of low birth; their primary object was to make their own fortunes, and, to promote the interests of their employers as well as their own, the poor islanders were made their victims. None of them were kept as domestic servants; and pains even were taken to make them sink under their burdens, because, in virtue of the king's orders, others could be forced to take their places. The governor-general not daring to refuse anything to the planters, still less to punish their unblushing cruelty, it is impossible to compute the number of the unhappy people who in a few months were sacrificed to the avarice of the grandees of Spain and of their agents. This explanation, which appears in the history of St. Domingo, by Charlevoix, shows clearly that nothing could be more inexcusable, nothing more cruel in practice, nothing that set all laws human and divine more at defiance than the actual government of the Spaniards in the West Indies.

Las Casas was stung to the quick at the sight of so much injustice, especially as he clearly saw that it would be the greatest of all obstacles to the conversion of the natives. Among many subjects of sadness, he had at least one consolation—that of finding the Dominican Friars imbued with the same sentiments of zeal that animated himself. They did not confine themselves to a mere approbation of his generous sentiments; they likewise gave many effectual and signal proofs of Christian charity and fortitude. They saw with heartfelt grief that irreligion was added to avarice; for the Indians, not being allowed sufficient time for instruction in the mysteries of our holy faith, were generally baptized, adults as well as infants, without any knowledge of the sacraments they received. The zeal of the missionaries was inflamed by this unchristian conduct, and they resolved to oppose it unceasingly with that manly freedom which has since immortalized their names. We shall relate the facts of the case in the very words of the celebrated Father Charlevoix of the Society of Jesus, in his history of the island of St. Domingo.

"The Dominican Fathers," says he, "were the first to open their eyes to the injustices that were practised. Four of them had lately come from Spain who soon became celebrated on account of their consistent piety and rigid austerities. They denounced existing abuses, especially usury, with great warmth. In a short time a visible improvement had taken place in the colony. They instituted catechetical instructions at regular hours for the children of the colonists and for the natives, and in the latter they found a degree of docility which delighted them. Having labored successfully to abolish the spiritual slavery of Satan, they failed even to mitigate the temporal slavery instituted by their countrymen among the natives. They denounced the system of repartimientos in no measured terms; but no sooner did they touch upon this delicate subject than the respect they had justly acquired was turned into violent persecution.

In Book V. of the same work we read as follows: "In the meantime the aboriginal inhabitants began gradually to disappear; and, although it was easy to foresee the loss the colony would sustain by their destruction, their cruel taskmasters, far from relenting in their wicked course, seemed bent upon their complete extermination. King Ferdinand, deceived by interested parties, although he had previously enacted wise and just laws in regard to the natives, seemed now to abandon them to their fate. He permitted that no compensation need be given them except food and clothing on condition, however, that their masters would annually pay to the royal treasury one *paros* for each Indian. The Dominican Fathers bitterly opposed this regulation; it would form, they said, an insuperable barrier to the conversion of the natives, and would render them less profitable withal to the Spaniards than they would be under better treatment. No regard was paid to these remonstrances, and the zealous preachers resolved to arm themselves finally with all the severity of their ministry in order to repress, by spiritual weapons, a scandal that caused the name of the Lord to be blasphemed among the infidels.

"In this resolution, Father Antonio de Montesino, a preacher of great sanctity and eloquence, ascended the pulpit of the church of St. Domingo, and, in presence of the Lord Admiral, Don Diego Columbus, of the royal treasurer, of several other persons of rank and of a very numerous auditory, declared the government of repartimientos to be unlawful. He added that the term *tutelage*— a term devised as a cloak for tyranny, concealed a direful slavery, to which, contrary to the laws of God and of men, an innocent people had been subjected; that this conduct, so contrary to the spirit of Christianity, had already brought destruction upon thousands of human beings for whom an answer should be made before God, and that this conduct would inevitably depopulate whole provinces of which the God of nations had given dominion to the Catholic sovereigns of Spain solely in order to bring all their inhabitants to the sweet subjection of the Christian gospel.

"Language of this kind failed not to wound the auditors most sensibly, and great murmurs were soon heard on all sides. It was even urged that he should be reprimanded as having shown a want of respect to the king himself as well as to those who governed in his name. A committee was accordingly appointed to wait upon Father Cordova, Prior of the Convent of Dominicans, in order to obtain redress. To their great surprise he declared that Father Montesino had said nothing in his sermon that was not true or that he should not have said; that all the religious of his order were of the same opinion; and that the sermon, about which they had made so much ado, was a matter preconcerted among the fathers. This was information they were very ill prepared to receive, and assuming a higher tone they observed that it was quite inconceivable that private persons having neither character nor position in the island should have had the boldness to condemn publicly what had been established by the counsels of wise men and sanctioned by sovereign authority; in a word, that Montesino should retract from the pulpit what he had asserted, or else the Dominicans should leave the island. The Prior heard them patiently; and, pretending to be moved by their threat, informed them that on the next Sunday Father Montesino would do all in his power to satisfy them.

"A great concourse accordingly assembled on the next Sunday—the self-love of many being doubtless gratified with the idea of hearing an apology to themselves for the previous Sunday's discourse. The preacher was well prepared; he commenced by saying that if the ardor of his zeal had, in his first sermon, prevented him from weighing his expressions sufficiently, he hoped that those who had taken offence would pardon him, the more especially as his zeal was in a just cause. He acknowledged that respect was due to those whom the king had made the depositaries of his authority, but that they were greatly deceived if they considered him guilty of any crime in raising his voice against the actual government of the repartimientos. His present sermon was of the same tenor as the former, though much more severe. Having entered into a very pathetic detail of existing abuses, he asked: What right had persons who could hardly have obtained a decent livelihood in Spain to consume the substance of a people as free as themselves? By what law could they dispose of these people as if they had been mere property and not human beings? What authority had they to treat them with such bitter cruelty? Would they never set bounds to that sordid avarice which had produced so many crimes? Did they wish to sacrifice to it fifteen or twenty thousand miserable Indians— the sad remnant of a million of souls whom they had found on the island on their arrival?

"Conduct so intrepid soon convinced the royal officers that nothing was to be gained by farther remonstrances, and that it was necessary now to lay the whole affair before King Ferdinand. Passamonte* rendered himself particularly conspicuous at this stage of the proceedings; he wrote to the king, and entrusted his letter to a Franciscan named Alphonsus D'Espinar, who was also authorized to make any verbal explanations necessary.

---
* The royal treasurer.

"The Dominican Fathers were not ignorant of what was going on, and as they were aware that several persons powerful at the court of Spain, and even some of the ministers of State, had an interest in sustaining the system of Indian repartimientos, they despatched Father Montesino himself to Spain to plead in person before the king the cause of the poor Indians. The good father found the whole court and even King Ferdinand predisposed to treat him with contempt. His eloquence, however, soon obtained for him a favorable hearing in the royal presence. The king soon discovered that, hitherto, his information on Indian affairs had been grossly deceptive. The wary monarch, always slow to decide according to first impressions, assembled a council of State in which both parties pleaded their respective causes with much warmth. Those who spoke in favor of the Indians insisted strenuously upon the principle that *all men are born free*, and that it never was permitted to any Christian nation to deprive of their liberty a people from whom they had received no wrong.*

---

* The Dominican theologians, such as Dominic de Loto and Francis de Victoria, were unanimously in favor of this view of the case. Mr. Hallam, in his history of Literature (vol. i., page 324, New York edition) mentions in terms of the highest praise the noble independence and profound erudition

"The other party opposed these great principles by arguments more plausible than solid—arguments by which no just man allowed himself to be deceived. The Indians, it was argued, ought to be regarded as children incapable of taking care of themselves; an Indian at the age of fifty was less advanced in knowledge, even of the most common things, than a Spaniard at the age of ten. It was well known that they remembered the simplest truths only as long as they were under instruction; that they could not remember the shortest prayer if they were not forced to recite it every day; that great pains had been taken to convince them of the indecency of living in a state of nudity, and that clothes were given them in abundance, but as soon as they were out of sight of their masters they tore them into pieces and ran to the woods, abandoning themselves to all manner of crimes. In their minds, sovereign happiness consisted in doing nothing; and this continual idleness, not to speak of the other crimes it produced, was the chief source of that indifference which they mani-

---

of these two writers, especially the latter, in maintaining international right. He gives credit to Victoria for having opened the way for Grotius in this important department of science.

fested, even in religious matters; finally, it seemed almost certain that the liberty which some persons would wish to give them would only serve to add to the foibles and incapacity of *children* the vices of corrupt *men*."

Even supposing these assertions to be true, the Dominican Fathers had still good reasons for urging their complaints. They could say with truth that the Indians did not get sufficient time to prepare themselves for the sacraments; that, in fact, many had been baptized without the least instruction or probation. But we will follow still further our faithful historian: "There may have been," continues Charlevoix, "some truth in the assertions of Montesino's opponents. That there was much exaggeration he easily succeeded in proving. But the great difficulty was that in giving absolute liberty to the Indians, the Spaniards would be reduced, in a short time, to the state of indigence from which they had emerged. This is another instance of the general axiom that what is just and true in law is seldom acted upon in politics. As it was necessary, however, to make some concessions to manifest equity of a cause so ably defended by the Dominicans, the king, *to satisfy his conscience*, decreed that the clause in the *last will* of Queen Isabella which provided for the just treatment of the Indians should be more faithfully executed; it was expected that this concession, meagre as it was, would satisfy all parties.

"In another provision it was declared that the Indians were *free* and should be treated accordingly, but that the repartimientos should remain in their present condition; two things, it will easily be seen, scarcely compatible. Also that, as beasts of burden had become quite numerous in Hispaniola, it was expressly provided that the Indians should be forced no more to carry excessive burdens, nor be punished for their offences by whipping. It was also ordained that *visitators* should be appointed, who were in some measure to act the part of protectors to the natives, without whose consent it would not be lawful to put them in prison. Finally, it was decreed that they should not be forced to work on Sundays or on festivals, and that women in a state of pregnancy should not be subjected to any kind of hard labor." These regulations were made in the year 1511.

CHAPTER III.

JOY OF LAS CASAS OVER THE SUCCESS OF MONTESINO.—
BAD FAITH OF THE AUTHORITIES IN ST. DOMINGO,
AND COLDNESS OF KING FERDINAND.—LAS CASAS
PUBLISHES THE DECREES HIMSELF.—TWO OF THE
DOMINICAN FATHERS DEPART FOR THE COAST OF
CUMANA WHERE THEY ARE SUCCESSFUL IN CON-
VERTING THE NATIVES.—THE PERFIDY OF A SPAN-
ISH CAPTAIN EXASPERATES THE INDIANS AND
CAUSES THE DEATH OF THE TWO FATHERS.—LAS
CASAS LABORS SUCCESSFULLY AMONG THE NATIVES
OF CUBA.—CONTINUED CRUELTIES OF THE COLON-
ISTS, AND DEPARTURE OF LAS CASAS TO SPAIN.—HE
IS PROMISED AN AUDIENCE.—DEATH OF THE KING.

THE regulations mentioned in the preceding chapter which, at best, could only mitigate the slavery of a people acknowledged to be free, were badly executed by the governors of the West India Islands. Las Casas, however, heard the tidings from Spain with singular satisfaction. He resolved to publish in person the royal ordinances, to have them executed if possible, and to oppose himself as a wall of brass to the violence and cruelty of which he continued to be an unwilling witness. If in the ardor of his zeal he then resolved to accomplish a good work, he never flinched in the execution of this resolution during the fifty-five remaining years of his life. Neither human respect, nor danger, nor labor, nor fatigue could make him relent in the least degree in that ardent zeal by which he was consumed. He labored night and day to procure the release of the natives of Hispaniola from bondage and their conversion to the true faith at the same time. Father Peter de Cordova, who had followed Montesino to Spain, became his zealous coadjutor in the same cause at the court of King Ferdinand. He ceased not to represent to his Majesty that his late ordinances, which ought to have been faithfully executed, were scarcely of any practical benefit to the Indians. After several consultations, Father Cordova was brought into the royal presence and received the king's assurances that he was convinced of the purity of his intentions, but that the advice of almost all the jurisconsults and theologians of the kingdom was to make no change in what had been established, but that he would take immediate action in regard to the disorders and abuses, the existence of which was a just cause of complaint. He advised the good father to return to his mission, and enjoined him and his brethren to inveigh no more against what was sanctioned by very wise persons; and informed him that the fathers might continue to enlighten and to edify the poor natives by their good doctrine and the sanctity of their lives as they had done hitherto, but that they should not interfere at all in the affairs of government. This discourse, so characteristic of the temporizing monarch, convinced Father Cordova that from the present aspect of affairs neither he nor his companions could hope to live in peace among their own countrymen in the New World, and that in order to effect any good among the natives they must seek a new field of missionary enterprise where no European would be likely to venture, and where they would, therefore, be alone with the natives. They accordingly petitioned the king to grant them permission and assistance to go to some distant shore upon which no Spaniard had yet set his foot, there to promulgate the blessed Gospel of Christ. He was pleased with the proposal, granted the necessary permission, and despatched orders to the admiral to furnish the missionaries with everything requisite in their holy enterprise.

Fathers Cordova and Montesino immediately set sail from Spain, and on their arrival in Hispaniola the admiral placed a vessel at their disposal, supplied them with all necessaries, and commanded the captain of the vessel to land them upon the coast of Cumana, on the northern shore of South America, which they had chosen as the first field of their apostolic labors. Father Cordova did not embark in the expedition, his presence being more necessary in St. Domingo, where, in accordance with the king's own orders, the Dominicans were put upon a better footing than before.

For the expedition were chosen Fathers Montesino, Francis de Cordova and John Garcez. The first-named fell sick at Porto Rico; and as his disease was of a dangerous and lingering character, his companions were obliged to continue their voyage without him. The spot upon which they disembarked was near the site of the future city of Coro, since called Venezuela or Little Venice, and it was in the year of our Lord 1512. They found an Indian village in the neighborhood where they were hospitably entertained by the inhabitants. They turned to good account the kindly disposition of the people by inducing them to embrace the Christian faith. Their words were heard with attentive respect, and they had every reason to promise themselves abundant success when the arrival of a Spanish vessel destroyed all their prospects. The object of the captain and crew was to capture and carry off the Indians and to sell them as slaves—an infamous commerce which became lamentably common in after years. As it was not the first attempt of the kind on the coast of Cumana, the natives were disposed to be on their guard; but the presence of the good fathers gave them confidence and they did not run to the woods as they had been accustomed to do on former occasions. The missionaries, who seem not to have suspected any evil design, entertained the ship's crew at a public festival—the Indians joyfully taking a part in it, and appearing very interested in promoting the enjoyment of their guests. Several days were spent in this friendly intercourse, when the captain of the ship invited the principal Cacique of the place to dine with him on shipboard; the invitation was accepted, but scarcely was the chieftain with his wife and about seventeen other Indians on board when the perfidious mariner set sail for St. Domingo.

On the first intelligence of this base and cruel perfidy our missionaries ran to the village, which they found in a violent state of excitement of which they expected themselves to be the victims. Strange to say, their virtues and the veneration in which these savages held them arrested, for the present, the expected stroke. The natives even allowed themselves to be persuaded that the two fathers had had no part in this foul treachery and that they had been totally ignorant of the whole plot. But the lives of the servants of God were not yet quite out of danger. At this juncture there appeared another vessel, the captain of which having landed seemed much affected by the tears of the natives and the critical situation of the missionaries, in which they could not answer for their lives one day. The fathers, on their part, to whom this officer appeared to be a good man, conceived some hope of escaping from the danger to which they were exposed. Heaven, they said, had sent him as their liberator; and they only asked of him the favor of conveying a letter, as soon as possible, to the admiral in St. Domingo. The captain was faithful to his charge; he soon arrived at his destination and presented himself before the admiral and Father

Cordova, explaining to them the whole affair. He conjured them to send back the captive Indians, as this was the only means of saving the lives of their friends.

The savages soon again became furious, nor were they to be appeased except on the condition that the captives of their nation should be restored to liberty in the space of four moons; if, at the expiration of that time neither vessel nor captive should appear, the missionaries were to suffer death. Letters were sent to Father Peter Cordova urging him to bring the matter to a speedy issue, but all their diligence was unavailing. The captives had already been sold when the letters reached St. Domingo, and even one of the officers of the royal audience had purchased them. The admiral had little or no authority over these officials, and neither the condition of the two religious, whose lives depended on the speedy liberation of the captives, nor the entreaties of their confrères, nor the infamy with which the guilty parties would cover themselves—nothing of all this could prevent the men whose duty it was to enforce the just decrees of the king from polluting themselves with the foul blot of being the indirect cause of the murder of two devoted priests. Thus it happened that, when the four moons or months had expired, and no tidings of the captives had been received, the missionaries were barbarously put to death.

Las Casas labored with different success in the island of Cuba. The natural docility which he found among the poor islanders delighted him, and he did not hesitate to proclaim publicly that it was much easier to induce the Indians to embrace the Christian faith in spirit and in truth than to prevail upon the Spaniards to lead a Christian life. His pure and disinterested zeal, his compassionate and ever active charity, and his firmness in resisting his countrymen in the abuse of their victories over the natives, so completely gained him their affections that they always clung to him with unbounded confidence as their greatest protector. "Thus," says Charlevoix, " he was able not only to convert the savages to the Christian faith, but also to render signal service to the Spanish colony, which, more than once, was in great peril of being smothered in its infancy, and could only have been saved from utter ruin by the authority he had obtained among the Indians."

When he learned what had taken place on the

coast of Cumana his soul was filled with sorrow. He mourned the loss of his two friends whose sanctity he had long venerated; he was grieved at the dishonor that had fallen upon the Christian religion; and his reflections upon what was taking place around him every day filled him with bitterness. From the sequel of this memoir the reader may easily judge of the disorders of which we speak. For if persons who in virtue of their very offices under government were more strictly bound than others to observe the royal ordinances trangressed them in the most essential provisions, it is easy to understand what little justice the poor Indians could expect in the Spanish colony.

Let us see what our faithful historian writes concerning the transactions of the year 1514: "The Indians were coupled together like beasts of burden, and having been forced to carry loads entirely beyond their strength they were urged forward by the lash. When they fell down from exhaustion they were obliged, by redoubled stripes, to get up again. A colonist, in ordinary circumstances, rarely went any distance from his house except when borne in a litter by two Indians. There was no scruple made of separating husband and wife—the man being sent to the mines from which he seldom returned, and the woman being employed in the cultivation of the lands. Whilst engaged in this severe labor they were all forced to live on roots and herbs. To see them die of such violence and of pure fatigue was an ordinary spectacle. Indian mothers who, on account of receiving no proper food, were unable to give suck to their children, often died with them of anguish and exhaustion.

"Another piece of cruelty surpassed, if it were possible, what has just been related. Some of the natives, to escape from this tyranny, ran to the mountains to conceal themselves. An officer was appointed whose business it was to chase them with dogs until they were found, but many were torn to pieces before the arrival of the officer. Many others, to escape so cruel a fate, drank of the juice of the *Cassada* plant—a deadly poison—or hung themselves from trees after having first rendered the same sad service to their wives and children. Such practices as these were of daily occurrence in the repartimientos; they were represented to the home government as absolutely necessary for the conversion of the people, and were even defended by certain doctors well informed as to the nature of the terrible details."

The Dominican Fathers saw these disorders, but had no power to prevent them; they perceived that the tyranny of their countrymen was likely to be perpetuated and that remonstrance on their part was useless. Las Casas, however, who could not keep silent on such a subject entered the lists against all abettors of the system of repartimientos. Being a man of extensive erudition, of solid judgment, of ardent disposition, of heroic courage which no difficulties could appal, he was immovable in his resolution when convinced it was for the glory of God. His having rendered important services both to the cause of religion and to the government in the island of Cuba gave him great credit in all the Indies. If fault he had, it was to give way occasionally to the promptings of a lively imagination and sometimes to show a disposition to severity against those whom he considered in fault.

He could not persuade himself that the king was rightly informed regarding the state of things in the New World, and judged it necessary to have a personal interview with him. He accordingly embarked for Spain, and arrived at Seville about the close of the year 1515. He immediately received letters of introduction to his Majesty from the worthy friar, Diego Deza,* the friend of Columbus, who was now Archbishop of Seville, and lost no time until he presented himself at the royal court which was then held at Placentia. Whilst presenting his letters to the king he took occasion to tell him that he had come from Hispaniola for no other purpose than to inform his Majesty correctly of what was done in regard to the native inhabitants of that island—a subject which affected equally, he remarked, the royal *conscience* and the royal *revenues;* and that he awaited the king's good pleasure to give full information on the whole subject. Ferdinand answered that his affairs did not then permit him to hear Las Casas, but that he would bear it in mind and give an audience as soon as possible. Las Casas, in the meantime, addressed himself to Father Matienzo, the king's confessor and a member of the Dominican order. Knowing that the king's guide of conscience was quite a

---

* Diego Deza holds a memorable place in the history of the discovery of America. He is the *worthy friar* of whom Irving writes, who, when Columbus pleaded his cause before the learned professors of Salamanca, was the first to adopt his opinions; and continued to the last the most steadfast friend the discoverer of America had in Spain.

power in the whole affair, he took care to inform him that Passamonte had sent letters against him (Las Casas) to the court; that the Bishop of Palencia and the commander, Lopez de Conchillos, had also used all their influence against him for the reason that *their* repartimientos in the Indies were more oppressed than any others; finally, that he could count on the assistance of no one at court excepting that of the good confessor himself whose aid he now implored. He then explained, at length, the cruelties perpetrated by the Spaniards in the West Indies, and conjured the reverend father in the name of God to undertake the defence of religion, justice and innocence.

Las Casas was not deceived in his man; Matienzo rendered a faithful report of what he had heard to the king, who sent word to Las Casas to meet him at Seville where they would have a lengthy interview. This answer revived his hopes, and the good father, who had already assisted him so much, now advised him to see the Bishop of Palencia, and Lopez, without whose counsel the king was not likely to decide upon anything. Lopez received him well, and gave him grounds to hope that nothing would transpire contrary to his wishes; but the bishop received him harshly and sharply rebuked him respecting his conduct. Las Casas hoped, however, that the favor of the Archbishop of Seville would out-balance the opposition of this prelate.

Having arrived at Seville, the first news he received was that King Ferdinand had died on his way thither, on the 23d of January, 1516. He was not disconcerted even by this unexpected news, as will be seen in the following chapter.

CHAPTER IV.

LAS CASAS PLEADS FOR THE INDIANS BEFORE CARDINAL XIMENES.—ENFORCEMENT OF THE OLD REGULATIONS AND ENACTMENT OF NEW ONES.—COMMISSIONERS APPOINTED TO GO TO THE WEST INDIES IN ORDER TO PROTECT THE NATIVE POPULATION.—LAS CASAS IS APPOINTED PROTECTOR-GENERAL OF THE INDIES.—MEANS ARE STILL CONTRIVED TO COUNTERACT HIS DESIGNS AND HE RETURNS TO SPAIN.

KING FERDINAND being now dead, Las Casas immediately formed the resolution of going to Flanders to give correct information to Prince Charles (Charles V.) on the state of affairs in the Indies before others could obtain a hearing on the same subject. Believing, however, that his success would be all the greater if he should make known his intentions to the celebrated Cardinal Ximenes, who had just been declared regent of Spain, he visited Madrid for the purpose, was kindly received by the cardinal who did not approve of his journey to Flanders. Ximenes gave him many special audiences, and finally heard him before a convention at which were present the Dean of Louvain, preceptor of Charles and afterwards Pope Adrian VI., as also Zapeta, Bishop of Avila, and the doctors Palacios Rubios and Carvagal.

In another assembly the statements of Las Casas were more carefully considered, and the cardinal produced a faithful copy of the instructions sent to Hispaniola in 1512 on the occasion of Montesino's visit to Spain. He then directed Las Casas to agree with Rubios upon some regulation by which the interests of the Indians would be secured and those of the Spaniards not entirely disregarded. It was an affair very difficult of adjustment. The deputies agreed upon a regulation which proposed three things: first, to instruct the Indians in the faith; secondly, to relieve them of some of their present burdens; and thirdly, to put them in a condition to pay to the crown of Castile the tribute which had been imposed upon them. To attain these ends it was agreed to separate the Indians from the Spaniards; to form a greater number of villages, and in each village to place a missionary with all the authority necessary to render his ministry useful and his person respected; also, to assign to each family a certain portion of land which was to be held perpetually and to be cultivated in the most profitable manner; finally, it was decreed to impose a tax proportioned to the nature of the soil and to the prosperity of the village. We will not give in detail the instructions delivered by Ximenes to the commissioners appointed to execute these regulations; it is undeniable, however, that avarice rendered them almost useless. Persons interested in preserving the system of repartimientos found fault with the regulations in Castile, and prevented their execution in the Indies. Cardinal Ximenes always listened with a willing ear to the proposals of Las Casas; and considering him necessary in the West Indies, conferred upon him an honorable office. He was appointed and named Protector-General of the Indies with a yearly salary of one hundred *pesos*, and received orders to accompany the commissioners to assist them by his influence among the natives and to inform them fully of all things necessary to be known. A ship was fitted out at Seville to carry them to St. Domingo, and all other vessels were strictly forbidden, for some time, to set sail for the Indies, lest, coming before the arrival of the commissioners, measures should be taken to counteract their instructions. This opportunity was also made use of to send several members of the Dominican and Franciscan orders as missionaries to the New World.

Notwithstanding the good intentions and precise orders of the great cardinal, little or no improvement was to be seen in the Indies. The commissioners either could not or dared not encounter so many difficulties.* Las Casas, with his accustomed charity, did all in his power to perform the part assigned him; but seeing the futility of his efforts, when greedy avarice reigned supreme, he resolved to return to Spain, again to plead the cause of the poor natives.

He set sail from St. Domingo on the 1st of May, 1517. He had already intended to bring a criminal process before the judges of appeal in Spain against those who, by their criminal neglect, had been the cause of the death of the Dominican Fathers on the coast of Cumana. Zuego, administrator of Indian affairs, before whom the case was to be tried, agreed in senti-

---

* These commissioners were three members of the Hierouymite order—Luis de Figueroa, Prior of La Majorada; Alonzo de Santo Domingo, Prior of the Convent of Ortega; and Bernardino Manzaneda. Inasmuch as they had never taken part in the controversies about the Indians, it was expected that they would act fairly to all parties.—*Translator*.

ment with Las Casas, but the trial could not be concluded without the concurrence of the Indian Commissioners, and thus the crime remained unpunished.

CHAPTER V.

LAS CASAS AT THE COURT OF CHARLES V.—HIS TRIUMPHANT APPEAL BEFORE THE EMPEROR AND ROYAL AUDIENCE IN FAVOR OF THE INDIANS.—HE IS SECONDED BY A FRANCISCAN FRIAR AND BY DIEGO COLUMBUS, ADMIRAL OF THE INDIES.—THE FORMER DECREES IN FAVOR OF THE INDIANS CONFIRMED.—OTHER ABUSES CORRECTED.—LAS CASAS OBTAINS A CHARTER TO TERRITORY WHERE HE IS TO ESTABLISH AN INDIAN SETTLEMENT ACCORDING TO HIS OWN PLAN.

GREAT changes had taken place in Spain since Las Casas had received his appointment of Protector of the Indies. Cardinal Ximenes was dead, and Charles V. having assumed the government of his vast dominions, a great number of Flemish noblemen, powerful at court, wished to obtain, after the example of the grandees of Spain, repartimientos in the Indies. The young king, not discerning all the consequences of their demand, granted it without difficulty. His liberality herein, which could only increase the evils for which a remedy had so long been sought, augmented also the anxiety and alarm of the protector of the Indies. Friends he doubtless had at court; but powerful enemies were not wanting. Many important affairs with which the king was then occupied, as well as the intrigues of those who were interested in keeping him in ignorance of the state of affairs in the Indies, always retarded the audience which Las Casas sought. Many other incidents, although not entirely breaking his patience, put it sorely to the test. In the meantime he proposed, and successfully carried into effect, various projects which tended to secure the welfare of the Indians. All depended, however, upon the practical carrying out of these projects in America; and, whilst his friends were laboring completely to attain this wished-for consummation, it was announced that Las Casas could have another audience with the king.

Don John de Queveda, a Franciscan, Bishop of Darien, had just arrived in Spain. It seemed that he had affairs of importance to bring before the royal council; and having sounded the feelings of that body, attached himself to Las Casas, who was evidently in favor with the Flemish lords and even with Charles himself. On a certain day the Bishop of Badajoz, one of the council of State, gave a dinner in compliment to the prelate lately come from America; Don Diego Columbus, admiral of the Indies, Don John Zuniga and Las Casas were also present. After dinner the conversation turned upon the Indians. Las Casas commenced by remarking that he felt conscious of having committed a fault in not bringing a writ of censure against the governor and other officers of the Indies, for refusing to carry out the ordinances of King Ferdinand respecting the cruelties inflicted upon the native population. The opinion of the Bishop of Darien being different, a warm discussion soon grew up between him and Las Casas. It was long and spirited, and was finally interrupted by the withdrawal of the host who was called away on business of importance. A full report of what had been said was soon transmitted by the Bishop of Badajoz to King Charles. Desiring only to be well informed on the subject, the king was glad of the opportunity of hearing two persons so likely to know the true state of the case, and so willing, withal, to express their respective views on the whole affair. He accordingly ordered the disputants to appear before him and his council on a certain day. The admiral of the Indies ano a Franciscan priest, lately come from Hispaniola, were also ordered to attend. On the day appointed Charles appeared in royal apparel and in unusual splendor. All the nobility of his suite took their places according to rank, and the chancellor, turning to the Bishop of Darien, addressed him in these words: " His Majesty, the king, Most Rev. Bishop, wishes you to express your sentiments regarding the manner in which the native inhabitants of America ought to be governed."

The bishop rose, and having made a lengthy preamble regarding the honor conferred upon him in being permitted to speak before so great a prince, he intimated that what he had to say was not of a nature to be communicated to any excepting the king and his privy council—hence, he begged his Majesty to have those persons present only whose duty it was to deliberate on affairs that ought to be kept secret. The chancellor informed him that all who were present belonged to the king's council, and that his Majesty wished him to proceed. He assented, but without entering into any details he told them in general terms that it was five years since he had first arrived in Terra Firma ; that during this period nothing had been done either for the advancement of religion or for the interests of the king ; that the colonies, instead of being prosperously established, were going to ruin ; that the first governor was a wicked man, the second still worse, and all of them were bad ; that his principal object in coming to Spain was to inform his Majesty of the true state of affairs.

When he came to the great point upon which his advice was required, he stated that all the Indians whom he had seen either in the country from which he had come or in those countries through which he had passed, seemed born only for slavery ; that they were perverse by nature, and that in his judgment they should not be left to themselves, but rather distributed through a country parcelled out into districts, and placed under the discipline of virtuous Spaniards. If this were not done all attempts to make them Christians or even men were in vain.

At the conclusion of this discourse Las Casas was ordered to reply, which he did in the following words : " Sire, I am one of those Castilians who first passed into the New World. I have been an eye-witness of the different species of conduct pursued by my countrymen in regard to the natives of America. Never would I come to a conclusion, nor properly would I avail myself of the honorable opportunity which your Majesty has given me, were I to enter into a detail of the horrors which I have myself witnessed, and of which I have been informed by persons in no manner likely to deceive. More than once have I already recounted those horrors to your Majesty and to your council. At present I will not repeat them, but I should betray the cause of innocence were I to neglect replying to what has been advanced by the illustrious Bishop of Terra Firma. In the first place, he could only have spoken of the inhabitants of his own province; and is it just to pass judgment upon all the Indian nations from his knowledge of one? Secondly, he reproaches the Indians with their vices; a little reflection on this subject, I am sure, will convince him that there are few of these vices they did not learn from the Spaniards. Again, it is said they are incapable of governing themselves; how then could they have maintained themselves so long under the government of their Caciques? Who has preserved them from such intestine commotions as have so often distracted the most flourishing and even the best governed States of Europe. Even supposing that to be true which should first be proved—that they stand in need of guardians, where are these to be found? Is it among the Spaniards? And how have *they* treated them up to the present time? Would not this be giving to wolves the care of lambs? Every inch of the New World resounds with the cries of men who suffer a more relentless cruelty than that of Nero or of Caligula. But they are born, it is said, for slavery, and from the earliest records of man they have been the mere slaves of their fellow-men. Let us not thus flatter our cupidity; let us not close our eyes upon our true relations with these people. All nations are equally free, and no nation can justly deprive another of liberty. Let us act in their regard as we would have them act in ours were they to land upon our shores with as great superiority of forces as we had over them upon the first discovery of the New World. Where is the difference? Has the *power* of the *strongest* a right to prescribe against *justice*? By what article of the Christian faith is this authorized?

"Moreover, is it not an unheard of method of preaching a gospel by which *we* have been raised to the liberty of the children of God, to reduce to the most cruel slavery a people born as free as ourselves; to scourge pitilessly with whips a people whose only crime in our regard is not to be able to bear the unjust and intolerable burdens imposed upon them; to inundate their own native soil with native blood; to deprive them of the necessaries of life, and to scandalize them by our excesses? All this has been carefully concealed from your Majesty; it is, however, what I have witnessed with my own eyes, and concerning which I cannot be deceived. Decide, I pray you, upon the cause of the Indians according to your judgment and your conscience, and I am convinced that they will joyfully submit to your decrees."

In this discourse the prominent feature is the noble zeal and love of justice so characteristic of Las Casas. If, as has been complained, he exaggerated the innocence and good behaviour of the Indians, it cannot be denied that his statements regarding the cruelties of the Spaniards were correct.

When Las Casas had finished his discourse, the Franciscan Father was next called upon to give his opinion. He began by saying that he had been twice appointed to make a census of the natives of Hispaniola; that at the time of the second census there was a decrease in the population of several thousands; that the decrease was growing more and more every day; and that, so far as concerned Hispaniola, the evil for which they sought a remedy seemed almost incurable. He feared that the measure of Spanish crime in the Indies was full to overflowing. He believed that God had not permitted this wholesale extermination of the Indians without cause, nor contrary to their true interests. "For," he continued, "when God said to Cain, 'the blood of your brother Abel cries from the earth to heaven for vengeance against you,' there was question of the death of only one man. Will this same Almighty Father then be deaf to the cries of those torrents of blood by which the vast Indian provinces are stained? Sire, I conjure you by the adorable wounds of the Saviour of men, by the sacred stigmas of my holy father, St. Francis, to put an end to this tyranny, the continuance of which cannot fail to draw down upon your crown the accumulated indignation of the Omnipotent ruler of kings and of men."

Don Diego Columbus, admiral of the Indies, was finally requested to give his opinion. He said that he had always disapproved of the repartimientos, and that if a speedy remedy were not applied to the evils of which Las Casas and the Franciscan Father had truly spoken, the Indies would soon be reduced to the condition of a barren desert; that his principal business in Spain at that time was to represent to his Catholic Majesty the true state of things in America, and he was convinced that it was a matter of the highest importance to settle all things relating to the Indians speedily and well.

It was a triumph and a subject of great consolation to the good Las Casas to find that all who spoke their minds candidly agreed in sentiment with him. Even the Bishop of Darien, being interrogated a few days later in regard to what he thought of the projects of Las Casas, said that he heartily approved of them. The commissioners sent to San Domingo previously to this time by King Ferdinand, had also acknowledged, though tardily, that the system of bringing the Indians together in villages was not only practicable but also necessary for their preservation.

Las Casas obtained another favor of the king in a private audience. He complained that under the pretext of carrying off the Carribean

Indians and of selling them into slavery on account of their cannibalism, many other Indians, entirely innocent of this crime, were also forced away. He mentioned especially the island of Trinidad, the inhabitants of which were very tractable, but would soon be entirely expatriated if not saved from such a cruelty by the interferance of royal authority. The king, profiting by this information, gave instant orders that all Indians reduced to slavery under pretext of cannibalism should be immediately set at liberty. Strong measures were also adopted to prevent such disorders in future. In an extraordinary assembly, the plan proposed by Las Casas for the establishment of a new colony was adopted; his title of Protector of the Indians was confirmed; and three hundred leagues of territory along the coast of the American continent were given him, where he might labor in accordance with his own peculiar views for the spiritual and temporal welfare of the natives. The last audience was given him in 1519 in which he obtained from his Majesty almost everything that he had sought for. Special marks of esteem were also shown him by the great lords of the court in which they followed the example of their sovereign.

CHAPTER VI.

FURTHER TROUBLES ON THE COAST OF CUMANA.—LAS CASAS ESTABLISHES A COLONY THERE WHICH IS RUINED THROUGH THE IMPRUDENCE OF HIS LIEUTENANT IN HIS ABSENCE.

LAS CASAS embarked at Seville in January, 1520, accompanied by two hundred laborers. The voyage was prosperous, but the news he received at the island of San Juan or Porto Rico, where he landed, was discouraging. Religious men of the orders of St. Dominic and of St. Francis had been established a short time on the coast of Cumana. As they had left their homes not to obtain the gold of the Indians, but to labor for their instruction in the Christian religion, their success was only equalled by their zeal. They soon gained the confidence of the natives, who heard them willingly, profited by their teaching, and were edified by their lives. This state of affairs had been quite encouraging to Las Casas, who intended to establish his colony in this same province. But, unhappily, an event not dissimilar to the one already mentioned disturbed the prosperity of the missions and destroyed all hope of success.

Alphonsus de Ojeda, having stolen away some Indians from the neighborhood of a village named Maracapana, had the imprudence to land at that village with his prey. The Cacique of the place, having attacked him from an ambuscade, cut him off with six of his companions. The rest of his followers escaped to their ship. This Cacique sent an account of what had happened to another chieftain whose village was only four leagues distant, and not very far from the small Dominican convent of Sante Fé. He advised him to put the inmates of the convent to the sword so as to rid the country entirely of Europeans and the disturbances caused by them. The suggestion was executed on the day following, which was a Sunday. The good religious, ignorant of the whole design, were massacred four or five leagues from their convent whilst one of them was preparing to say mass, and the other, who seems not to have been a priest, was making his confession. The savages, having stripped the convent and chapel of their ornaments, set fire to both.

Nothing was known of this last melancholy

event at San Domingo, when, on the news of the fate of Ojeda, it was immediately resolved to transport the entire population of Cumana to San Domingo and reduce them to slavery. The execution of this project was committed to Gonzalez de Ocampo, and he had just embarked with three hundred good and well-provisioned troops when Las Casas landed at Porto Rico. As soon as he arrived he was informed of the disaster which had taken place on the coast of Cumana and of the terrible vengeance which the Spaniards were preparing to take. Scarcely had he time to reflect upon the ill news when Ocampo himself entered the port. Las Casas immediately presented himself before the commander, who had been an old friend; showed him the provisions of his orders from the king, and endeavored to convince him that, in virtue of the powers with which he was invested, he alone had the right to take cognizance of what had taken place on the coast of Cumana. His arguments, however, and his powers were alike unavailing. Ocampo, after several protestations of friendship, informed him that he had also his own commission; that he had no power to make any change; and that all representations on the part of Las

Casas should be made to the admiral of the Indies and to the royal audience. On these terms they separated—Ocampo resolved to continue his voyage, and Las Casas, having left his laborers and all his effects at Porto Rico, determined to sail immediately for San Domingo. He found the admiral well disposed towards him; he had, therefore, no difficulty in procuring the registry and promulgation of his commission. We can well understand that the publication of the decrees was a very unpalatable measure to many of the colonists, but Las Casas still retained in his interests many sincere and powerful friends. His principal business in San Domingo now was to prevent the execution of the orders committed to Ocampo; his efforts here, however, were as ineffectual as they had been in Porto Rico. Ocampo, having landed first on the island of Cubagua, erected batteries on the mainland, and using strategem as well as force soon succeeded in his enterprise. A Cacique was killed, numbers of the principal Indians were either captured or slain; the Spanish ships were filled with captives, who were sent soon after as slaves to San Domingo; those of the villagers who implored pardon, obtained it; and the foundations of a city named Toledo were laid by the Spaniards.

Nothing could have been more prejudicial to the designs of Las Casas than this establishment; he had feared it when he first understood the purposes of Ocampo, and he had never desisted in his efforts to have that officer recalled. No attention was paid to his entreaties by the royal audience until matters had become hopeless. The auditors, having much more of the merchant in the composition of their character than of the magistrate, set up for sale justice itself. They dared not oppose directly the orders of the king, but they cunningly eluded the enforcement of them, now under one pretext and now under another. Las Casas, tired of such duplicity, threatened to return to Spain and inform the king of what had taken place. His menace had its effect; propositions were soon presented to him which he could, in conscience, subscribe; and he thought it better to do so than to expose himself to the danger of not succeeding at the court of Spain. In 1521 he signed a treaty which provided that a company should be organized of which any person then living in San Domingo might become a member. The same vessels that had conveyed Ocampo to the coast of Cumana together with one hundred and twenty-eight good troops to protect his infant colony, were also placed at his disposal. The little fleet set sail from San Domingo in July, and steered for Porto Rico, where Las Casas had left his laborers, but where none of them were now to be found. Some were dead, and others, satisfied to remain in Porto Rico could not be induced to travel any further. This was a grievous loss to him, inasmnch as he had borne all the expense of bringing these people together, as well as the expense of their voyage, and had suffered much anxiety and fatigue on their account. But his troubles did not terminate here. Having arrived at New Toledo, he there found the inhabitants so disheartened at the prospect of being obliged continually to carry on war with the natives, that they only awaited a favorable opportunity to abandon the settlement forever. This opportunity was offered by the arrival of Las Casas with his ships; he could not prevail upon them to engage in his project, and they all embarked for San Domingo, accompanied also by the troops who followed their example.

Any other man would probably have abandoned an enterprise against which so many obstacles seemed to conspire, but we have already had signal proofs of that indomitable perseverance which did not now desert him. By the aid of an Indian convert, named Mary, he communicated to the natives the fact that he had come with full powers from the King of Spain to put an end to the system of treachery and tyranny to which they had too long been subjected; and that his object now was to give them a knowledge of the true God, and with it all the blessings they could desire. His charity towards the poor people made him all to all; and in a short time he hoped to induce many of them to embrace the faith of Christ. There is no denying, however, that the inhabitants of this coast had their vices; their desire to obtain Spanish wines amounted almost to madness. Not content with what they could procure by means of their gold and other articles of value, they even made excursions through the country with a view to take away other Indians and sell them to the Spaniards for wine. Whilst the wine lasted they were never sober, and it is easy to imagine to what an extent savage men in a state of drunkenness indulged in all sorts of crimes. This traffic, so unjust in itself, so pernicious in its effects, could not long escape the notice of Las Casas. The worst aspect of the case was that those who, according to the royal ordinances, were obliged to obey Las Casas, were always ready to disobey him if their personal interest required it. Even the governors of provinces were conspicuous in this opposition. The governor of Cubagua, for instance, absolutely refused to enter into his views; and Las Casas resolved to complain of him to the royal audience at San Domingo. If they failed to do justice, he would bring the affair before the court of Spain.

At his departure he left his little colony under the direction of a certain Francis de Soto (not the discoverer of the Mississippi) with two special orders: first, not to allow the two ships lying in port to be taken away on any account; secondly, that if the Indians should attack him in such force as that he could make no effectual resistance, he was to remove the colony to Cubagua with all their effects. The first of these orders Soto obeyed, imperfectly and he left himself in no condition to execute the second. Scarcely had Las Casas sailed out of sight when the two vessels of the colony were sent out in different directions in quest of gold, precious stones and slaves. The Indians, taking advantage of the defenceless condition of the little colony, fell furiously upon it, burned the town of Toledo and killed all the Spaniards that could not save themselves by flight. Soto, with certain religious of the order of St. Francis, perished in the number. The Indians, emboldened by success, next attacked the island of Cubagua, and the governor, although he could have put himself at the head of three hundred good troops, had not the courage to await an attack. Shamefully panic-stricken, he embarked precipitately for San Domingo, where he met the sad remnant of Soto's colony just arrived from the scene of their disaster. They all agreed in giving a most pitiful account of their misfortunes. Probably they left out the important circumstance that these sad reverses were the evident effect of the imprudence of Soto and the cowardice of the governor.

Las Casas had not yet arrived at the capital of San Domingo. Adverse winds having obliged him to put to shore on a distant part of the island, he pursued his journey by land and took the route of Leogana where he remained for some time. Having resumed his journey he met certain Spaniards on the road who seem to have come from the capital. Inquiring about the general news, they informed him that it was reported on good grounds that Bartholomew Las Casas and most of his colony had been massacred by the Indians on the coast of Cumana. Putting a few more questions to them he soon discovered all that had happened, and raising his hands to heaven he exclaimed: "Thou art just, O Lord! and Thy judgments are right." Arriving at the city of San Domingo, he found that all he had heard was but too true. Though sensibly affected he was not disheartened. His labors were all undertaken solely for the glory of God and the advancement of the Christian faith; and as he sought not his own interests and had done all that duty required of him, he had no difficulty in submitting cheerfully to the will of God. When he came to San Domingo, preparations were making to punish what was called the second revolt of Cumana. He advised the adoption of measures more conformable to the spirit of Christianity than those likely to be enforced, but he only met opposition, and saw in this case more clearly than ever that men who were slaves of avarice could never agree with a true minister of the Gospel either in the end to be attained or in the means of attaining it *

---

* It appears, upon the most reliable authority, that, in leaving his colony at that time, Las Casas did not act according to his own judgment. One of the Franciscan Fathers was continually urging him to go; and Las Casas, having held out a long time against his remonstrances, was at last prevailed upon to absent himself temporarily in order to obtain protection against the predatory visits of the Spanish vessels. "Hereupon we may remark," says Mr. Helps in his Life of Las Casas, "that a man seldom makes so signal a blunder as when he acts exceptionally, and contradicts the usual tenor of his life and character."

CHAPTER VII.

LAS CASAS BECOMES A DOMINICAN.—LIVES EIGHT YEARS IN RETIREMENT.—BECOMES PRIOR OF THE CONVENT OF ST. DOMINGO.—GOES TO SPAIN TO OBTAIN FROM CHARLES V. REGULATIONS FAVORABLE TO THE INDIANS OF MEXICO AND PERU RECENTLY CONQUERED BY CORTEZ AND PIZARRO.—HISTORY OF THE CACIQUE HENRY.

LONG detached from the world and from those who followed its maxims, both in sentiment and conviction, Las Casas now resolved to consecrate himself to God in some religious order. His preferences were long in favor of the order of St. Dominic, and in the year 1522 he sought and obtained admission among the brethren as a novice. The great affair of his salvation seemed now to absorb all his thoughts. He lived in strict retirement and in the perfect fulfillment of his duty as a religious. Little is known of him during this time, and he is hardly heard of except when new occasions called forth his zeal in the conversion of the Indians. When he received the habit of St. Dominic he was in his forty-eighth year;

eight years, counting from that date, he spent in his convent at San Domingo, always regulating his life by the example of the most holy religious and zealous missionaries. He spent his nights in prayer and study, and most of the day in seeking out the poor Indians among the forests and mountains, consoling them in their afflictions and preparing them for baptism. Father Peter de Cordova, having terminated a holy life by a happy death in 1525, Las Casas was entrusted with the government of the Dominican convent. To him it was certainly a position, though humble in a worldly sense, honorable and congenial, for this convent had always been the bulwark of Christian faith, of justice and of charity in the island of San Domingo.

When, in 1530, the report gained credence that the Spaniards, having made new discoveries, were preparing for new conquests, Las Casas took the alarm, concluding with good reason that the natives of the newly-discovered lands would be subjected to all the cruelties and injustice of what was called the law of conquest. When justice and humanity were jeopardized, we have seen that Las Casas knew no difficulty. Another instance of his unflinching charity now appeared. Once more he made a voyage to Spain to obtain of the emperor, Charles V., laws more rigorous, more precise, and better calculated to save the Indians from violence than any laws enacted heretofore. He presented to the emperor and his council a memorial entitled: *The Destruction of the Indies by the Spaniards*, in which he always speaks only of what he had himself witnessed, but which was of itself sufficient to fill with horror even the most effeminate courtiers.

This memorial, written with as much spirit as truth, drew from Charles V. another edict in favor of the Indians. Fortified with this edict and with the power also to enforce it, he immediately set sail for San Domingo, intending to pass thence into Mexico and Peru as soon as possible. Before leaving San Domingo, however, he desired to render a much-needed service to the colony by stifling the last sparks of the long and unhappy war which had been commenced and carried on by the Cacique Henry, whose history we shall here briefly relate.

Queen Isabella had strongly recommended a system of education for the Indians suited to their capacity, and that as soon as their minds were enlightened and their hearts formed to virtue there should be given them some employment of which they were capable. But in this, as in many other things, her instructions had not been followed. The sons of Caciques, although they had learned the language and adopted the religion and customs of the Spaniards, and had even acquired a knowledge of the Latin language, were regarded in the repartimientos as no better than the least of their subjects; were, in fact, scarcely distinguishable from them except in being more bitterly persecuted. Of these young and noble Indians there was one named Henry, whose ancestors had held sway in the mountain districts of Baoruco. He had embraced the Christian religion in good faith and as a matter of free choice, and was endowed with many noble qualities. The wisdom of his mind appeared in his manners, and his happy expression of countenance made a very favorable impression. In his whole deportment were visible the effects of a refined education, and he certainly did not merit by his conduct the fate of a slave. He bore his hard lot without a murmur, and faithfully served a master who seems to have shown him some kindness. Upon the death of his first master, however, he fell into strange hands—into the hands of a galley officer, a cruel and relentless tyrant and debauchee, who, having inflicted all injuries upon him, spared not even the honor of his wife. Henry often complained of this treatment to the tribunals, but his complaints only rendered his condition more intolerable. He was scornfully driven off by the magistrates without a hearing, and his task-master only redoubled the severity of his treatment.

In this state of irritation he readily listened to the suggestions of other Indians whose lot was little different from his own, that, if he would put himself at their head, they would follow him through all vicissitudes of fortune until they should recover their liberty, or sell their lives in the attempt at the dearest rate. He accepted the dangerous command, furnished his followers with such arms as he could find, and betook himself to a post in the mountains of Baoruco, in which he was secure from any surprise. Valenzuela, a Spanish captain, was no sooner informed of their flight than he put himself at the head of about a dozen men to pursue them and reduce them to obedience. Having discovered their retreat he was preparing for the attack, when the

Cacique, advancing towards the Spaniards, calmly informed them that neither he nor his followers could ever be brought back, nor should they again be slaves of the Spaniards. The captain, enraged at this declaration and despising an enemy of whose character he was ignorant, ordered his soldiers to seize him. The Indians immediately fell with fury upon the Spaniards, killed two of their number, and put the rest, of whom some were wounded, to an inglorious flight. Valenzuela, being himself severely wounded and unable to proceed, fell into the hands of Henry, who dismissed him with these words: "Go, now, and give thanks to God that I have spared you, and if you are wise you will not return." The news of the affair soon spread, abroad and the ever vigilant royal audience believed that it was necessary to use all their power to crush out the rebellion in its inception. Eighty soldiers, under good officers, were ordered to pursue the fugitives and bring them to reason before they could fortify themselves. Henry, apprised of these preparations, was not slow to put himself in a condition to receive his enemies. He intrenched himself in the woods, before which the Spaniards soon appeared. Without giving them time to reconnoitre he attacked them briskly, soon threw them into confusion and gained a complete victory. Many of the soldiers were slain, but such as escaped the slaughter and fell into Henry's power were treated with moderation. This action had very different effects on the parties concerned; the Spaniards began to discover that they had to deal with men, and the Indians to realize the fact that their oppressors were not invincible. In a short time Henry found himself at the head of three hundred trusty followers. Having trained and equipped them as well as he could, he soon rendered these poor islanders, long regarded as no better than mere animals, terrible to the conquerors of his country. The manner of warfare was peculiarly honorable to the Indians, for they never allowed themselves to pass beyond the limits of simple defence. Companies of Spaniards continued to be sent out against them who were always defeated, and the captives treated leniently. Henry's self-control was especially remarkable on one occasion. Having defeated a considerable number of Spanish troops, many of whom fell in battle, there remained sixty-one, who, to avoid falling into the hands of the enemy, hid themselves in a cave in the hope of escaping by night. They were discovered in their hiding place by some of the Indians who surrounded the cave, and, having carefully closed all its apertures with combustible matter, were preparing to set it on fire. At this moment Henry arrived; he sharply rebuked his men on account of their cruel designs, and, satisfied with disarming the Spaniards, gave them liberty to go where they pleased. Thus it was that having overcome his enemies in bravery, he seemed still more desirous of surpassing them in generosity. He deserved no more praise for his vigilance than he did for the wise measures which he adopted in the government of his republic. Deserts, into which the Spaniards had never dared to penetrate, were rendered habitable to men. The lands were cultivated by the men who were unable to bear arms and by the women. Herds of cattle browsed along the fields; poultry flourished; and hounds were kept to chase the guinea pig. Abundance reigned where once had been a frightful wilderness, whilst Henry, with fifty trusty followers, watched the approach of the enemy. He frequently visited all the outposts, and vigilantly guarded the avenues through which the Spaniards might enter. The fame of his success had spread over all the colonies, and it was not doubted that he could act on the defensive for a long period. This little war, commencing in 1519, was not ended till 1533. The Spaniards had often had recourse to negotiation, and had sent to the Cacique religious men and officers of distinction instructed to make a treaty on the most favorable terms. They were always received with a degree of courtesy which was all the more honorable to the Cacique, as some of the ambassadors had been actually engaged in the enslavement of his relatives. The assurances given him of pardon for the past, and freedom from compulsory labor in the future, could not, however, induce him to deliver up himself and his followers to those who had not kept faith with them since their arrival in the island. His answer was that he would make no attack except in case of self-defence; that he only strove to maintain his freedom in the mountains; and that he knew not by what right the Spaniards sought to subject him to their rule. He also assured them that he would steadfastly adhere to the Christian faith, and that he had never made Christianity responsible for the crimes of those who made profession of it.

In the meantime his troops increased day by day—the Indians, and the Moors also who dwelt amongst the Spaniards, continued to swell his ranks. Had Henry been ambitious of conquest he could have destroyed the colony at any moment. The colonists, aware of their danger, left no means of an accommodation untried. As negotiation and the sword had alternately been tried to no purpose, it was now resolved to have recourse to the emperor, whose advice or intervention it was hoped would bring about a speedy settlement of the difficulties. The politic prince did not think it unworthy of his high station to write to the Cacique, promising many advantages in case of a treaty of peace, and his royal word for the faithful fulfilment of its provisions. An officer of rank, named Barrio Neuvo, was made the bearer of this letter and was empowered to sig i a treaty with Don Henry, as he was styled by the emperor. The officer left San Domingo with thirty soldiers and as many Indians who we e to act as guides through the mountains. Having travelled with great difficulty for several days through mountain defiles almost impassable, they were informed that Henry was not a great distance from them, but that in order to reach his habitation it was necessary to pass through a swamp in which the water would probably reach their hips, and then to cross another mountain still more difficult of ascent than those they had already passed over.

De Barrio, having advanced so far that retreat itself was a matter of difficulty, endeavored to extricate himself as best he could. In the first place he found means of sending to the Cacique a letter advising him of the emperor's commission. Henry despatched one of his relatives to compliment him, and to tell him that he would confer with him on the questions at issue at his own wild home in the mountains. De Barrio was, therefore, obliged to continue his journey. The road was difficult enough, but to make matters worse, the Indian who had acted as principal guide to the expedition led him through places so rough and craggy that they were often obliged to use their hands as well as their feet in climbing over the rocks. The wearied soldiers often murmured a wish to retrace their steps, and argued that the Cacique, in inviting him to advance, either mocked him or was plotting his ruin. The indomitable Spaniard had taken his resolution however, and whatever fate awaited him he was resolved upon executing the emperor's orders. He told his followers that he had not forced them to come with him, and that those who did not choose to keep him company might return. But at last he arrived at the Indian settlement and was received by Henry with every mark of respect and even of sympathy in his destitute condition. A conversation upon general topics was entered into, but in a short time the main question was opened up. The Spanish officer began as follows:

" The emperor, my most august sovereign and yours, the most potent monarch in the world, yet the mildest of rulers, who regards his subjects as his children, could not have learned the sad condition of affairs in San Domingo and not be moved by sentiments of compassion. The evils you have inflicted upon the Castilians, his first and most faithful subjects, irritated him not a little. But when he understood that you were a Christian, and endowed, besides, with many noble qualities, his anger was dispelled, and his whole desire was to induce you to accept good and reasonable terms. He has sent me, therefore, to exhort you to put an end to this war, and to grant you and all your followers a full pardon for the past. But if you persist in your rebellion, I am commanded to pursue you until your forces shall have been vanquished, and troops sufficient to effect this purpose are placed at my disposal. You are not ignorant of what it has cost our good emperor to send me here—all this he has done for your sake, and I am ready to expose myself to every danger to carry out the instructions of my sovereign and to do you a service. On this account I had no fears in delivering myself into the hands of one in whom there dwells no sentiment unworthy of his birth or of his religion, whose moderation is known to all, and who is fully capable of drawing a proper distinction between those who come as friends and those who come to deceive."

Henry listened attentively to this discourse and received with due respect the emperor's letter in which assurances were given him that orders had been issued to the royal audience to the effect that if he and his followers would submit to the royal authority in good faith, lands should be granted to them where they could enjoy their liberty and live in abundance. He received at the same time the safe-conduct of the royal audience bearing the seal of the chancellor, and having examined it he said that he had always loved peace and that it was the force of necessity alone which impelled him to go to war; that, if he had hitherto rejected all measures of accommodation, it was because he could not trust men who had so often broken faith. "Now," he added, "since his imperial Majesty gives me his word, I stand indebted to him and accept with gratitude the favor he has conferred upon me." He had no difficulty in obtaining the consent of the other Indians—a treaty was soon concluded, and numerous protestations of sincere and enduring friendship were made on both sides. This treaty was concluded in the year 1533, the war having lasted fourteen years. The Spanish officer returned to San Domingo, accompanied by an Indian captain named Gonzalez. who, on the part of Henry, was to represent his cause before the royal officers and auditors, and to observe closely all their movements to see if some treachery were not still lurking in their councils. Gonzalez witnessed the universal joy which the news of the treaty diffused through the capital of the island; he listened to the praises lavished on the prudence, courage and zeal of De Barrio, and finally beheld the solemn ceremonies which accompanied the promulgation of peace. The attentions, however, paid to Gonzalez, in order to dispel all suspicion of bad faith, prevented him from returning as soon as he expected, and the delay gave rise to a suspicion in the mind of Henry that he might be again put to the necessity of putting himself in an attitude of defence.

Las Casas had then just returned from Spain, and the treaty of peace concluded with his dear Indians filled him with joy and gave a new stimulus to the zeal of which he had already given so many proofs. He visited the Cacique Henry, to whom he was well known, and the mountains of Baoruco resounded with shouts of joy on the arrival of the great Protector of the Indians. Las Casas profited by these good dispositions to open his heart to those whom he so tenderly loved and who so fully reciprocated his affection. He made known to them all that had taken place in their favor, dwelling especially on the goodness of the emperor who had, in a certain degree, compromised his dignity in order to find out the place of their abode, so that their souls might no longer be exposed to ruin by living in a condition in which all means of practising the duties of a Christian life were wanting. On the subject of religion he had reason to be edified, for the Cacique assured him that nothing had given him so much pain as seeing, during the war, numbers of children die without baptism, and numbers of adults die without the other sacraments. This consideration, he continued, had induced him above all others to consent to a treaty of peace, even although he had not yet any certain assurance that the step was not fraught with evil to his people. He had never neglected his regular daily devotions, and he strictly observed the fast of Friday. It was admitted even by his enemies that he had watched vigilantly over the morals of his people and that he had never tolerated suspicious intercourse between persons of a different sex. Las Casas prolonged his stay in the mountains, and succeeded in dispelling the fears of the Cacique respecting the intentions of the Spaniards. His words were implicitly believed by the poor Indians, and the man of God found the greatest docility in them all. He said mass for them often, baptized their children, and prepared their adults to receive holy communion. He found among his neophytes great ignorance even of the most essential articles of our holy religion, but his patient zeal soon supplied a remedy for this evil. Having convinced them that their fears of the bad faith of the Spaniards were groundless, he drew from them the promise that as soon as their present stock of provisions should be exhausted they would descend from their mountain fastnesses and execute the treaty in due form.

The royal audience had manifested their displeasure on hearing that Las Casas had gone among the Indians without their knowledge; on hearing of his success, however, their alarm was turned into joy. He certainly had cause of consolation, in this instance at least, in the conduct of both parties. Don Henry, as he was now called, arrived with all his suite in San Domingo where he solemnly ratified the treaty which had previously been signed only by his deputies. The Spaniards, on their part, received him in a manner well calculated to gain his confidence; permission was given him to establish himself and his whole nation, of which he was the hereditary chief, in any province he might choose; they were exempted from tribute, and only required to acknowledge the sovereign authority of the emperor and of his successors, the kings of Castile. Soon after, the Caciques formed a settlement in Boya, distant nortwestwardly three or four leagues from the capital. All Indians who could trace their descent to the aboriginal inhabitants of the island had permission to follow him, and about four thousand availed themselves of the privilege. Their descendants down to the eighteenth century, we are told, enjoyed the privileges granted to their forefathers.

CHAPTER VIII.

LAS CASAS VISITS MEXICO, PERU AND OTHER PROVINCES TO PUBLISH IN THEM THE DECREES OF THE EMPEROR IN FAVOR OF THE INDIANS.—WITH SOME OF HIS BRETHREN HE CONQUERS TO THE FAITH THE "LAND OF WAR."—HE GOES TO SPAIN AGAIN.—IS APPOINTED FIRST BISHOP OF CHIAPA.—HIS DIFFICULTIES AS BISHOP.—RESIGNS HIS SEE.—RETURNS TO SPAIN FOR THE LAST TIME.—HIS CONTROVERSY WITH SEPULVEDA.—HIS DEATH.

OUR zealous missionary now set sail for Mexico in order to publish in the newly-conquered countries the decrees of the emperor. His principal object was to impress them upon the minds of those who commanded the armies in those regions. If full conformity with the commands of the emperor was not effected in all places, there can be no doubt that his decrees were respected in many, and it certainly was not the fault of Las Casas if any remained ignorant of their true purport. He traversed the vast provinces of Mexico or New Spain, the kingdom of Peru, Guatemala and the neighboring provinces, everywhere exercising the double functions of missionary apostolic and protector of the Indians. Having entered with some of his brethren the region known as La Guerra or Land of War, he effected a strict compliance with the edicts of the emperor, and this circumstance greatly promoted the conversion of the natives.* He signally failed, however, to find in the conquerors of all the provinces the same good dispositions. Most of them, blinded by the lust of gold, seemed to have lost every sentiment of humanity. Cruelties as great, sometimes even greater, than those which disgraced the first discoverers of the New World were perpetrated daily in Mexico. The zeal of the servant of God increased in proportion to the difficulties against which he con-

* A beautiful Life of Las Casas has lately been published in London, written by Arthur Helps, in the ninth and tenth chapters of which there is a lengthy account of the conversion of the natives of the Land of War. The principal agents in this work, after Las Casas, were his brethren of the Dominican order, Luis Cancer, Pedro de Augulo and Rodrigo de Ladrada. They first learned, as perfectly as possible, the language of the country; and then having put into versé and set to music the principal mysteries of the Christian religion, they committed the verses to merchants who traded with these Indians, and who faithfully performed their part by gaining the attention and good-will of the natives for the doctrines contained in them. The Cacique expressed a desire to see the reverend fathers, and Luis Cancer was sent to him. He was received with marks of honor everywhere, and was eminently successful in his mission. Las Casas and Pedro de Augulo then started for the field of missionary enterprise, and in a short time the whole nation received the faith. This was in 1537 and 1538. The region had been a terror to the Spaniards.—*Translator.*

tended ; and it places his sincere piety in the strongest light that in all his labors, journeyings and fatigues he never allowed himself any relaxation in the observance of his rule—never neglected his accustomed exercises of prayer and study. Nicholas Antonio tells us that the short intervals of repose granted to him in the convents of his order in Mexico were carefully devoted to the study of the best works on theology and the best commentaries on the Holy Scriptures.

About this time he formed the strictest friendship with the Bishop of Guatemala, Francisco de Marroguin, at whose request he undertook another voyage to Spain. Arriving in Castile in 1540, he there learned that Charles V. had just gone to Germany. It was an untoward event ; but his charity did not allow him long to remain inactive. The monstrous crimes of which he desired to complain had now come to the knowledge of all Europe ; he gave an exact account of them to the royal council of the Indies ; and, when the emperor returned, he urged his cause with so much zeal as to obtain of his Majesty new edicts and regulations in favor of the Indians.

As a consequence of these decrees he demanded and obtained the liberation from abject bondage of a great number of Indians in Spain; and the emperor, always his friend, gave now another proof of his good-will by naming him first Bishop of Chiapa, the principal place in a province of the same name in Mexico. This dignity was refused, as formerly had been that of the bishopric of Cusco in Peru. All his friends, and especially his brethren of the Dominican order, advised him to accept it; and considering the influence which the episcopal character would give him in repressing the vices of his countrymen and in causing the laws favorable to the Indians to be better observed, he was at length prevailed upon to accede to the wishes of the emperor and the Pope. His acceptance was, however, accompanied by the express condition that he should have the privilege of visiting all the Indian provinces in order to free them from any oppression they might suffer; but, as this condition was not considered compatible with the episcopal character, he was obliged reluctantly to relinquish it. Pope Paul III., having erected Chiapa into an episcopal see appointed Las Casas its first bishop, and he was accordingly consecrated in the cathedral of Seville on Passion Sunday, in the year of our Lord 1544, being then in his sixty-eighth year.

With characteristic zeal he entered upon the discharge of his duties as bishop. Neither his advanced age, nor the vast extent of his diocese, nor the dangers of the sea, nor the persecutions of powerful enemies whose principal object was to conceal their crimes, could in the least degree mitigate his ardor. Before leaving Spain he had induced several members of his own order, animated with the desire of promoting the glory of God and the salvation of men by the exercise of the holy ministry, to accompany him to the New World. Having procured two vessels for the transportation of the Indians, liberated at his own request in Spain, he spent the whole time of the voyage in teaching them their religious duties, and in impressing upon their souls the love of God. The late edict of the emperor had been published in all the conquered provinces, and he had good reason to hope that the condition of the natives would be notably improved. In this hope he was once more disappointed. By present as well as by past experience he was convinced that men who had been long accustomed to violate, without scruple and with impunity, the laws of God and of nature in regard to their fellow-men, would easily find pretexts for violating the commands of their sovereign when they could do it with safety.

The famous conquerors of Mexico and Peru, blinded by a career of brilliant success, believed that it was lawful, as a reward of their extraordinary daring, to treat the conquered natives as they pleased. The immense quantities of gold sent by them to Spain, the magnificent accounts of the conquests lately achieved, the pains taken to employ venal scribes to publish pompous treatises on the benefits accruing to the monarchy from the services of these warriors, shielded the guilty for a time from the just indignation of the emperor. Moreover, the distance from Spain to the new countries was so great, and the duties of his Majesty so multiplied, that he could scarcely devote sufficient time to examine their conduct strictly, or to weigh the complaints brought against them. Under these circumstances little regard was paid to the remonstrances of the holy bishop. More than once was he threatened with personal violence ; sometimes he received from Spanish officers, civil and military, treatment similar to that which St. Paul received from Jews and Gentiles ; and proof in abundance remains to show that he imitated the conduct of that holy apostle no less in patience and mildness than in courage and firmness. He had no fears for the safety of his life; it was long since he had devoted it entirely to the service of God. Contempt, humiliation and evil treatment he regarded as appendages of his ministry; and he considered it an honorable privilege to suffer something for the sake of Jesus Christ. His life was often threatened; imprisonment was also hinted at; but the Word of God could not be enchained, and it was always powerful enough in his mouth to put his enemies to silence and often to strike terror into the hearts of those who attempted to intimidate him.

He spent much time in the instruction of his priests. Knowing by long experience what the life of a missionary among the Indians ought to be, he was particularly assiduous in impressing upon the minds of his clergy the course of conduct to be pursued in treating with the Indians and also with those Spaniards who wished to play the tyrant among them. His own conduct was a model in this particular. With the greatest familiarity he instructed the poor natives, spending much of his time in making them acquainted with the principles of our holy religion. Forcibly, yet charitably, did he reform the vices of his countrymen. To all that knew him, whether Indians or Spaniards, the regularity of his own life and the practice of every Christian virtue was a constant subject of edification. Thus did he lay the foundations of Christianity in the diocese of which he was the first pastor. More delighted with the thought of having gained a soul to Christ than others were with having made themselves masters of all the gold of Peru, he did not envy their groundless pleasure. The only favor he demanded of them was to set bounds to their cupidity and not to destroy the fruit of his ministry by a continual re-enactment of the cruelties by which the whole country was defiled with blood. These cruelties, he constantly maintained, gave the simple natives the most plausible reason to say that a religion professed by such monsters as committed them could not be from God. Certainly they would have had reason to say so if Christianity had authorized the conduct of such Christians. But they were often incapable of making a just distinction between faith and practice. To remedy this evil our zealous prelate added to his familiar instructions various writings adapted to the state of all classes of Christians.

In these he explained the purity of gospel morality, as well for the benefit of those who suffered as of those who inflicted persecution. He thus conveyed to the minds of the natives a higher idea of our holy faith, and to the Spaniards he gave an opportunity of reading the condemnation of their own lives in his simple exposition of the truth.

Never, perhaps, since the days of the apostles did any of their successors suffer greater contradictions. If he had only to combat the errors, infidelity and ignorance of men to whom the name of Christ had hitherto been unknown, he might have had reason to hope for a successful accomplishment of his wishes. But when an entire army, composed for the most part of bad Christians, spread around them the deadly poison of wicked example, and seemed to glory even in the commission of crimes that would put the pagans themselves to shame, we can form a correct idea of the difficulties which stood in his way. In order the better to devise the surest means of preventing the evil effects of such example he held conferences with other bishops recently arrived in Mexico, and when he found it expedient he also appeared before the civil tribunals to procure a more rigid enforcement of the laws and to plead for the oppressed. It was a sore affliction to him to see that almost all his efforts were unavailing, and that the oppressors of America, not content with having scandalized and robbed his poor Indians, seemed bent upon destroying them totally, murdering, without the least formality, princes and private persons, men, women and children.

So heavily did this desperate state of affairs weigh upon his mind that he resolved to resign his bishopric. He put his design into execution, according to Father Echard, in 1547, but according to Nicholas Antonio, in 1551.

It is with reluctance that we have so frequently referred to the cruelties with which Las Casas has filled volumes. We feel certain, however, that he cannot be accused of having outstepped the limits of truth inasmuch as he was an eye-witness of most of the facts he narrates, and especially as he published his writings in Mexico under the very eyes of the guilty parties, and then presented them repeatedly in Spain to the emperor and his council. Moreover, he is not the only witness in this cause. Holy missionaries, such as Cordova and Montesino of the

Dominican order, and several members of the Franciscan order as well, complained bitterly of these excesses. The works of Nicholas Antonio, always sensitive to the honor of his native land (Spain), give unexceptionable testimony to the same effect. We do not think, however, that the scandalous crimes committed for the most part by the Spanish soldiery in the new world should be laid to the charge of the Spanish nation. We have certain knowledge, moreover, that the sovereigns of that nation, Ferdinand and Isabella, Charles V. and Philip II., far from authorizing these excesses, made stringent laws to prevent them; and that the same nation which sent forth men who destroyed the natives, sent forth also men whose apostolic zeal was worthy of the first ages of Christianity, and who fearlessly proclaimed themselves, under all circumstances, the defenders of the oppressed.

In a work of this kind it is impossible to enter into the details of the horrors committed; they were very great beyond a doubt. Some are of opinion, however, that they were occasionally exaggerated by Las Casas in his zeal to prevent their recurrence. The admission is not too much for common charity to make in favor of the conquerors of the New World. Be this as it may, the conduct of our holy bishop, an involuntary witness of crimes of the darkest hue, in denouncing them with so much force, often, too, in the presence of death itself, is a subject for universal admiration. That his life was not actually taken constitutes at least some excuse in favor of his enemies. His pathetic discourses, his writings, his prayers and tears being incapable of moving hearts as hard as adamant, he was convinced that nothing remained for him but to weep in seclusion and in solitude the sins he could not prevent. After having labored so many years in an ungrateful and painful mission; after having made himself not only the father and protector of the Indians, but also, in some measure, a martyr for their freedom; after having borne with a truly heroic courage the fatigues and dangers of so many voyages, and exposed himself to so many persecutions on the part of his countrymen, Las Casas sailed for the last time to Spain. He resigned into the hands of the sovereign pontiff the dignity with which he had been invested, and retired into a convent of his Order. Thus did he leave to those who sought them the treasures of Mexico and Peru, and carried with him in his retirement a higher treasure than this world can give—the consciousness of having devoted a long life to the cause of justice, truth and humanity.

But in separating himself from a people he ardently loved, he did not, at the same time, resign the liberty of speaking, writing and acting in their favor. Hence it was that he chose the convent of Valladolid as his place of retreat. Here the court of Spain principally resided, and here also was the voice of Las Casas often heard in behalf of his poor Indians. The occasion for contradiction soon offered itself. John Genez de Sepulveda, a native of Cordova and canon of Salamanca, one of the ablest writers of his time, undertook the defence of the conquerors of the New World. True, he had never been in America, but he certainly could not have been entirely ignorant of the crimes committed in that country. And the suspicion still attaches to his memory that he had been prevailed upon by the friends of the conquerors, perhaps by their gold also, to write a work in Latin, entitled: "The Justice of the War of the King of Spain against the Indians."

He presented his work to the royal council and used every means to have it published. But Las

Casas, aware of his design, and persuaded that such a work would be a scandal to religion, inasmuch as it would seem to justify the greatest crimes of which men could be guilty, opposed its publication with equal zeal. The Archbishop of Seville was of the same opinion, and earnestly demanded its suppression. The royal council, believing that it was the business of theologians to settle these disputes among themselves, referred the whole subject to the universities of Alcala and Salamanca. Both faculties decided in favor of Las Casas, and, having examined the work, declared that the doctrine contained in it was dangerous and unsound. Francis de Victoria, the celebrated Dominican writer on the laws of nations, had already given his individual opinion to the same effect. In the meantime, Sepulveda was very urgent with the emperor to have his book published. Failing in this he sent his manuscript to Rome, where no one knew anything about it, with a request to a special agent there to have it printed secretly. The emperor, irritated by the dishonesty of the measure, strictly forbade the circulation of the work in his dominions, and caused all the copies of it that could be found to be immediately destroyed. His vigilance however, did not prevent a number of copies of the work from finding their way into Spain, and it was soon translated into the vernacular tongue. This drew from Las Casas a masterly reply, in which he successfully established the truth of his principles. But the redoubtable Sepulveda did not give up the contest. Persuaded that it would be dishonorable in him to concede the point in dispute, he obtained permission of the emperor to have a public disputation with Las Casas, who, true to his character, cheerfully accepted the challenge. Dominic de Soto was named umpire, and the discussion lasted several days before the royal council. The venerable bishop addressed himself to committees of the council, and then demanded that his reasons should be committed to writing and presented to the emperor. Soto drew up a summary of the principal arguments on both sides, and Nicholas Antonio tells us that notwithstanding all the eloquence and erudition of Sepulveda, who was called the Spanish Cicero, Las Casas convinced the council that it was neither just in itself nor in its circumstances to oppress or to reduce to slavery the natives of the West Indies. Charlevoix here remarks that many of the council were of opinion that *actual* settlers should not be disturbed in the possession of their lands, and that the slaves of whom they then held possession should remain with them in quality of hired servants. This measure was also reprobated by Las Casas, who declared it impracticable, and urged that to leave them in the power of Spaniards in any way was to sacrifice them to cruel avarice.

About this time he wrote his famous tract entitled: "The Tyranny of the Spaniards in the Indies;" a work printed some years later, and dedicated to Philip II.* We could wish that many of the crimes therein related had been buried in oblivion till the great accounting day, "but," as Charlevoix says, "we may rest assured that the holy Bishop of Chiapa, whose name, notwithstanding his defects, or to speak more correctly his excess of virtue, shall live forever with renown in the annals of the New World as well as in the history of Spain, did not foresee the effects produced by his work a few years later. It was soon translated into French, and during the war between Spain and Holland was circula-

---

* It is important to note this fact, as it shows that the Spanish government was always willing to be well informed on Indian affairs, and ever ready to apply a remedy to existing evils.—*Translator.*

ted extensively among the people of the latter country and stimulated them more than anything else to achieve their independence, fearing lest, if they made a treaty with Spain, the same cruelties awaited them as had been inflicted upon the Indians." At the present time few will admit this, even if it were true, as a charge against the character of Las Casas. It is also true that the cruelties practised in the Indies had long been published and well known in all parts of Europe; and if the work of Las Casas caused the evil complained of, it was owing entirely to the imprudence or bad faith of those who undertook to defend what was wrong in itself.

The holy bishop spent the last fifteen years of his life for the most part in prayer and retirement, but he never abandoned the cause of the Indians, in whose favor he ceased not to interest himself as long as he lived. His long and checkered career, so faithfully and so persistently devoted to works of pure and noble charity, drew at last to a close. In the month of July, in the year 1566, in the city of Madrid, full of merits and of days, he calmly reposed in the Lord.

In the records of Christianity we cannot find a name distinguished by a more disinterested devotion to a noble object than that of Las Casas. Almost fifty years of his life were spent amid the hardships and privations of a missionary life in a newly-discovered country and among a people till then unknown by Europeans. With the spirit of a Christian hero he braved every danger in pursuit of the one great object of his life—in advancing the spiritual and temporal interests of this rude and savage people. This object was pursued, too, in opposition frequently to those from whom he had reason to expect a hearty co-operation. Even the last years of his life were devoted to the same grand object, and a life such as his requires no eulogy. The actions of such a man, faithfully recorded, form the best eulogy that can be written.

Almost all his writings are on the same subject. Some of them are preserved in manuscript in the archives of the royal council of the Indies. Most of them were frequently printed and translated into different languages. We discern in all his works not only that strong feeling of justice and that unbounded zeal which so much distinguished him, but also a remarkable degree of eloquence and erudition. He founded his maxims invariably on passages of the civil and canon law and on the decisions of the best authors. If, even after his death, he had powerful adversaries, their efforts entirely failed either to gain the public esteem or to tarnish the great name against which they were directed. "Thus," says Nicholas Antonio, "Las Casas always remained victorious in the field of controversy he had chosen."

APPENDIX.

I.

[It has been customary to take it as a matter of course that Las Casas gave his unqualified assent to the practice of stealing negroes in Africa and reducing them to slavery. The following extract from the "Life of Columbus," by Washington Irving, vol. iii., page 416, New York, 1866, furnishes a very different version of that subject.]

Attempts have been made to decry the consistency, and question the real philanthropy of Las Casas in consequence of one of the expedients to which he resorted to relieve the Indians from the cruel bondage imposed upon them. This occurred in 1517, when he arrived in Spain on one of his missions to obtain measures in their favor from the government. On his arrival in Spain he found Cardinal Ximenes, who had been left regent on the death of King Ferdinand, too ill to attend to his affairs. He repaired, therefore, to Valladolid, where he awaited the coming of the new monarch Charles, Archduke of Austria, afterwards the emperor Charles V. He had strong opponents to encounter in various persons high in authority, who, holding estates and repartimientos in the colonies, were interested in the slavery of the Indians. Among these, and not the least animated, was the Bishop Fonseca, president of the council of the Indias.

At length the youthful sovereign arrived accompanied by various Flemings of his court, particularly his Grand-Chancellor, Doctor Juan de Selvagio, a learned and upright man, whom he consulted on all affairs of administration and justice. Las Casas soon became intimate with the chancellor, and stood high in his esteem; but so much opposition arose on every side that he found his various propositions for the relief of the natives but little attended to. In his doubt and anxiety he had now recourse to an expedient which he considered as justified by the circumstances of the case.* The Chancellor Selvagio,

---

* Herrera clearly states this as an expedient adopted when others failed. "Bartolome de las Casas, viendo que sus conceptos hallaban en todas partes dificultad, i que las opiniones que tenia por mucha familiaridad que havia seguido i gran credi to con el gran Canciller, no podian haber efecto, *se volvio a otros expedientes*, &c."—Decad. 2, L. 2, c. 2.

and the other Flemings who had accompanied the youthful sovereign, had obtained from him, before quitting Flanders, licenses to import slaves from Africa to the colonies; a measure which had recently in 1516 been prohibited by a decree of Cardinal Ximenes while acting as regent. The chancellor, who was a humane man, reconciled it to his conscience by a popular opinion that one negro could perform, without detriment to his health, the labor of several Indians, and that therefore it was a great saving of human suffering. So easy is it for interest to wrap itself up in plausible argument! He might, moreover, have thought the welfare of the Africans but little affected by the change. They were accustomed to slavery in their own country, and they were said to thrive in the New World. "The Africans," observes Herrera, "prospered so much in the island of Hispaniola that it was the opinion unless a negro should happen to be hanged he would never die, for as yet none had been known to perish from infirmity. Like oranges, they found their proper soil in Hispaniola, and it seemed ever more natural to them than their native Guinea."*

---

* Herrera, Hist. Ind. L. 2, D. 3, c. 4.

Las Casas, finding all other means ineffectual, endeavored to turn these interested views of the Grand-Chancellor to the benefit of the Indians. He proposed that the Spaniards resident in the colonies might be permitted to procure negroes for the labor of the farms and the mines, and other severe toils which were above the strength and destructive of the lives of the natives.* He evidently considered the poor Africans as little better than mere animals; and he acted like others, on an arithmetical calculation of diminishing human misery, by substituting one strong man for three or four of feebler nature. He, moreover, esteemed the Indians as a nobler and more intellectual race of beings, and their preservation and welfare of higher importance to the general interest of humanity.

It is this expedient of Las Casas which has drawn down severe censure upon his memory. He has been charged with gross inconsistency, and even with having originated this inhuman traffic in the New World. This last is a grievous charge; but historical facts and dates remove the original sin from his door, and prove that the practice existed in the colonies, and was author-

---
* Herrera, Hist. Ind. D. 2, L. 2, c. 20.

ized by royal decree, long before he took a part in the question.

Las Casas did not go to the New World until 1502. By a royal ordinance passed in 1501, negro slaves were permitted to be taken there, provided they had been born among Christians.* By a letter written by Ovando, dated 1503, it appears that there were numbers in the island of Hispaniola at that time, and he entreats that none more might be permitted to be brought.

In 1506 the Spanish government forbade the introduction of negro slaves from the Levant, or those brought up with the Moors, and stipulated that none should be taken to the colonies but those from Seville who had been instructed in the Christian faith, that they might contribute to the conversion of the Indians.† In 1510 King Ferdinand, being informed of the physical weakness of the Indians, ordered fifty Africans to be sent from Seville to labor in the mines.‡ In 1511 he ordered that a great number should be procured from Guinea and transported to Hispaniola, understanding that one negro could perform the work of four Indians.§ In 1512 and '13

---

* Herrera, Hist. Ind. L. 3, c. 8. † Idem. D. 1, L. 6, c. 20.
‡ Idem, D. 1, L. 8, c. 9. § Idem. D. 1, L. 9, c. 5.

he signed further orders relative to the same subject. In 1516 Charles V. granted licenses to the Flemings to import negroes to the colonies. It was not until the year 1517 that Las Casas gave his sanction of the traffic. It already existed, and he countenanced it solely with a view to having the hardy Africans substituted for the feeble Indians. It was advocated at the same time and for the same reasons by the Jeronimite friars, who were missionaries in the colonies. The motives of Las Casas were purely benevolent, though founded on erroneous notions of justice. He thought to permit evil that good might spring out of it; to choose between two existing abuses, and to eradicate the greater by resorting to the lesser. His reasoning, however fallacious it may be, was considered satisfactory and humane by some of the most learned and benevolent men of the age, among whom was the cardinal Adrian, afterwards elevated to the papal chair, and characterized by gentleness and humanity. The traffic was permitted; inquiries were made as to the number of slaves required, which was limited to four thousand, and the Flemings obtained a monopoly of the trade, which they afterwards farmed out to the Genoese.

Dr. Robertson, in noticing this affair, draws a contrast between the conduct of the cardinal Ximenes and that of Las Casas, strongly to the disadvantage of the latter. "The cardinal," he observes, "when solicited to encourage this commerce, peremptorily rejected the proposition, because he perceived the iniquity of reducing one race of men to slavery, when he was consulting about the means of restoring liberty to another; but Las Casas, from the inconsistency natural to men who hurry with headlong impetuosity towards a favorite point, was incapable of making this distinction. In the warmth of his zeal to save the Americans from the yoke, he pronounced it to be lawful and expedient to impose one still heavier on the Africans."*

This distribution of praise and censure is not perfectly correct. Las Casas had no idea that he was imposing a heavier, or so heavy a yoke upon the Africans. The latter were considered more capable of labor, and less impatient of slavery. While the Indians sunk under their tasks, and perished by thousands in Hispaniola, the negroes, on the contrary, thrived there. Herrera, to whom Dr. Robertson refers as his authority, assigns a

---
* Robertson, Hist. America, p. 3.

different motive, and one of mere finance, for the measures of Cardinal Ximenes. He says that he ordered that no one should take negroes to the Indias, because, as the natives were decreasing, and it was known that one negro did more work than four of them, there would probably be a great demand for African slaves, and a tribute might be imposed upon the trade, from which would result profit to the royal treasury.* This measure was presently after carried into effect, though subsequent to the death of the cardinal, and licenses were granted by the sovereign for pecuniary considerations. Flechier, in his life of Ximenes, assigns another but a mere political motive for this prohibition. The cardinal, he says, objected to the importation of negroes into the colonies, as he feared they would corrupt the natives, and by confederacies with them render them formidable to government. De Marsolier, another biographer of Ximenes, gives equally politic reasons for this prohibition. He cites a letter written by the cardinal on the subject, in which he observed that he knew the nature of the

---

* Porque como iban faltando los Indios i se conocia que un negro trabajaba mas que quatro, por lo qual habia gran demanda de ellos, parecia que se podia poner algun tributo en la saca, de que resultaria provecho a la Rl. Hacienda. Herrera Decad. 2, L. 2, C. 8.

negroes; they were a people capable, it was true, of great fatigue, but extremely prolific and enterprising; and that if they had time to multiply in America they would infallibly revolt and impose on the Spaniards the same chains which they had compelled them to wear.* These facts, while they take from the measure of the cardinal that credit for exclusive philanthropy which has been bestowed upon it, manifest the clear foresight of that able politician, whose predictions with respect to negro revolt have been so strikingly fulfilled in the island of Hispaniola.

Cardinal Ximenes, in act, though a wise and upright statesman, was not troubled with scruples of conscience on these questions of natural right, nor did he possess more toleration than his contemporaries towards savage and infidel nations. He was grand inquisitor of Spain, and was very efficient during the latter years of Ferdinand in making slaves of the refractory Moors of Granada. He authorized, by express instructions, expeditions to seize and enslave the Indians of the Caribbee islands, whom he termed only suited to labor, enemies of the Christians, and cannibals.

---

* De Marsolier, Hist. du Ministere du Cardinal Ximenes, Lib. 6. Toulouse, 1694.

Nor will it be considered a proof of gentle or tolerant policy that he introduced the tribunal of the inquisition into the New World. These circumstances are cited not to cast reproach upon the character of Cardinal Ximenes, but to show how incorrectly he has been extolled at the expense of Las Casas. Both of them must be judged in connection with the customs and opinions of the age in which they lived.

Las Casas was the author of many works, but few of which have been printed. The most important is a general history of the Indias, from the discovery to the year 1520, in three volumes. It exists only in manuscript, but is the fountain from which Herrera, and most of the other historians of the New World, have drawn large supplies. The work, though prolix, is valuable, as the author was an eye-witness of many of the facts, had others from persons who were concerned in the transactions recorded, and possessed copious documents. It displays great erudition, though somewhat crudely and diffusely introduced. His history was commenced in 1527, at fifty-three years of age, and was finished in 1559, when eighty-five. As many things are set down from memory, there is occasional inaccuracy, but the whole bears the stamp of sincerity and truth. The author of the present work, having had access to this valuable manuscript, has made great use of it, drawing forth many curious facts hitherto neglected; but he has endeavored to consult it with caution and discrimination, collating it with other authorities, and omitting whatever appeared to be dictated by prejudice or overheated zeal.

Las Casas had been accused of high coloring and extravagant declamation in those passages which relate to the barbarities practised on the natives; nor is the charge entirely without foundation. The same zeal in the cause of the Indians is expressed in his writings that shone forth in his actions, always pure, often vehement, and occasionally unseasonable. Still, however, where he errs it is on a generous and righteous side. If one-tenth part of what he says he "witnessed with his own eyes" be true, and his veracity is above all doubt, he would have been wanting in the natural feelings of humanity had he not expressed himself in terms of indignation and abhorrence.

In the course of his work, when Las Casas mentions the original papers lying before him, from which he drew many of his facts, it makes one lament that they should be lost to the world. Besides the journals and letters of Columbus, he says he had numbers of the letters of the Adelantado, Don Bartholomew, who wrote better than his brother, and whose writings must have been full of energy. Above all, he had the map formed from study and conjecture by which Columbus sailed on his first voyage. What a precious document would this be for the world! These writings may still exist, neglected and forgotten among the rubbish of some convent in Spain. Little hope can be entertained of discovering them in the present state of the cloister. The monks of Atocha, in a recent conversation with one of the royal princes, betrayed an ignorance that this illustrious man was buried in their convent, nor can any of the fraternity point out his place of sepulture to the stranger.*

The publication of this work of Las Casas has not been permitted in Spain, where every book must have the sanction of a censor before it is committed to the press. The horrible picture it

---

* In this notice, the author has occasionally availed himself of the interesting memoir of Mon. J. A. Llorente, prefixed to his collection of the works of Las Casas, collating it with the history of Herrera, from which its facts are principally derived.

exhibits of the cruelties inflicted on the Indians would, it was imagined, excite an odium against their conquerors. Las Casas himself seems to have doubted the expediency of publishing it; for in 1560 he made a note with his own hand, which is preserved in the two first volumes of the original, mentioning that he left them in confidence to the college of the order of Predicators of St. Gregorio, in Valladolid, begging of its prelates that no secular person, nor even the collegians, should be permitted to read his history for the space of forty years; and that after that term it might be printed if consistent with the good of the Indias and of Spain.*

For the foregoing reason the work has been cautiously used by Spanish historians, passing over in silence, or with brief notice, many passages of disgraceful import. This feeling is natural, if not commendable; for the world is not prompt to discriminate between individuals and the nation of whom they are but a part. The laws and regulations for the government of the newly-discovered countries, and the decisions of the council of the Indias on all contested points, though tinctured in some degree with the bigo-

---

* Navarrete, Collec. de Viag. T. 1, p. lxxv.

try of the age, were distinguished for wisdom, justice and humanity, and do honor to the Spanish nation. It was only in the abuse of them by individuals to whom the execution of the laws was intrusted, that these atrocities were committed. It should be remembered also that the same nation which gave birth to the sanguinary and rapacious adventurers who perpetrated these cruelties, gave birth likewise to the early missionaries, like Las Casas, who followed the sanguinary course of discovery, binding up the wounds inflicted by their countrymen; men who, in a truly evangelical spirit, braved all kinds of perils and hardships, and even death itself, not through a prospect of temporal gain or glory, but through a desire to meliorate the condition and save the souls of barbarous and suffering nations. The dauntless enterprises and fearful peregrinations of many of these virtuous men, if properly appreciated, would be found to vie in romantic daring with the heroic achievements of chivalry, with motives of a purer and far more exalted nature.

II.

APOSTOLIC LETTER OF POPE PAUL III., A. D., 1537, DECLARING THE AMERICAN INDIANS TO BE RATIONAL CREATURES.

PAUL III., pope, to all the faithful of Christ who shall see the present letters, health and apostolical benediction.

Truth itself, which can neither deceive nor be deceived, when it appointed the preachers of faith to the office of preaching, is well known to have said: *Go, teach all nations.* He said *all* without any distinction, for all are capable of receiving the instruction of the faith. The enemy of mankind who always opposes good undertakings in order to bring them to nought, aware of this commission, and instigated by envy, invented a method hitherto unknown of preventing the Word of God from being preached to the nations that they might be saved. As he has excited some of his satellites, who, eagerly desiring to satisfy their avarice, habitually *presume* to assert that the Western and Southern Indians and the other nations which in these times have come to our knowledge, under the pretext of their being devoid of the Catholic faith, should, like brutes, be brought under our servitude—and, indeed, they are made slaves and treated with an inhumanity that their masters would scarcely exercise over the very brutes that serve them;—we, therefore, who, though unworthy, are the vicegerent of our Lord upon earth, and who seek with our whole endeavor the sheep of his flock entrusted to us and who are outside of the fold, in order to bring them into the fold itself, reflecting that these Indians as true men are not only capable of the Christian faith, but also, as has been made known to us, that they embrace the faith with the utmost promptitude, and wishing to provide them with suitable remedies, decree and declare by apostolical authority that the above-mentioned Indians and all other nations who may in future come to the knowledge of Christians, though they be out of the faith of Christ, can freely and lawfully *use, possess and enjoy their liberty in that regard; and that they ought not to be reduced to slavery; and that whatever may otherwise have been done is null and void.* Moreover, that those Indians and other nations are to be invited to the aforesaid faith of Christ by the preaching of the Word of God and by the example of a good life. This decree is to hold good, notwithstanding any previous acts and whatsoever else to the contrary.

Given at Rome, iv. *non.* Jun., 1537, the third year of our pontificate.

www.ingramcontent.com/pod-product-compliance
Lightning Source LLC
Chambersburg PA
CBHW031354160426
43196CB00007B/804